THE GUITAR MAKER'S WORKSHOP

The *Guitar Maker's* Workshop

Rik Middleton

The Crowood Press

First published in 1997 by
The Crowood Press Ltd
Ramsbury, Marlborough
Wiltshire SN8 2HR

British Library Cataloguing-in-Publication Data
A catalogue record for this book is available from the British Library.

ISBN 1 86126 040 7

Acknowledgements
David Dyke has given me a great deal of support and encouragement
and the opportunity to pick his brains. In addition, his infectious
enthusiasm for his material has been one of the seminal influences in
my involvement in instrument making.
   Adrian Farmer has been most generous with his knowledge and
practical help.
   'Mags' Bissell has been skilful enough to retrieve my photography.

Typeset and designed by
D&N Publishing
Membury Business Park, Lambourn Woodlands
Hungerford, Berkshire.

Printed and bound in Great Britain by
WBC, Bridgend, Mid Glam.

Contents

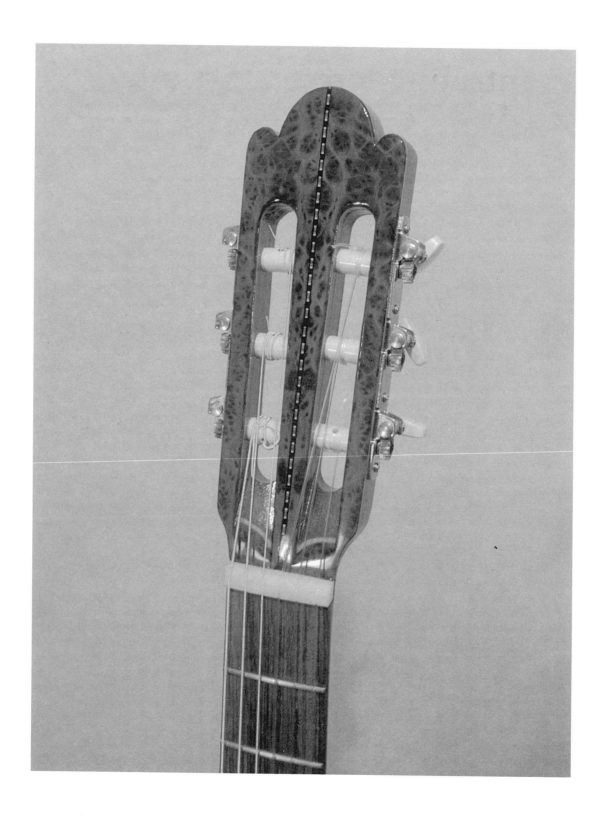

1 Introduction to the Guitar Maker's Workshop

I want to do more than show you how to make a guitar. I want to introduce you to the whole ethos and approach of the luthier's workshop: the thoughts and feelings of the processes and the ways in which they differ from the work of the cabinet-maker and of the wood-turner. It does seem to me that guitar making requires a different state of mind, although this is very difficult to put into words.

I relate it to my first experience of woodwork and metalwork in secondary school. Metal was smooth and reliable but it did take ages to cut and to file. Wood was nasty splintery and very unreliable stuff and they expected me to be able to cut it into interlocking shapes which would match together. I remember a very low success rate at this and appealing to my woodwork master 'Couldn't we just glue it together instead of trying to make all these complicated joint things?' Now, ironically, I have come through the complex processes of cabinet-making to luthiery. Luthiery is nothing if not exacting work but in traditional guitar building there are no joints. Planed surfaces are glued together without interlocking. There are consequences: the metal G-cramps so useful in binding many cabinet-maker's joints together while glue

Some of the work starts at the drawing board.

dries, here cause problems. Many other old friends in the tool rack lie accusingly redundant while other newcomers have taken up their places alongside.

That there is a major difference of approach is, I think, shown by the cabinet-makers I know who have turned to luthiery and been successful only to give it up and return to cabinet-making, perhaps for the greater variety of processes and techniques that are involved. I find it very difficult not to make instruments; having to make furniture now is something of a frustration.

So how to capture and convey this difference in working in luthiery? The luthier's workshop is, of course, suffused with the aroma of a variety of timbers. There is Pine but there is also more than one variety of Cedar. There is scented Cypress. There is Rosewood which, when worked, gives off its characteristic smell somewhere between roses and old-style tobacco. All these are mixed with vapours of various finishing materials and other solvents. One thing which does not vary, in my experience, is the fine layer of dust on anything that hasn't been used or cleaned recently.

The tooling in evidence shows some examples which people do not immediately associate with woodworking. There are scalpels. There is a rack of chisels and gouges typical of the cabinet-maker who might occasionally embellish his work with some carving, but alongside this there is a rack of artist's palette knives and a jar of brushes one might associate with a watercolour artist. There is a drawing-board and fair range of draughtsman's tools. There is a pile of thin ply templates and guards in a bewildering array of shapes and sizes. There is a rack of sticky tapes and sheet materials graded according to no obvious criteria. There is a box full of wooden wedges. Further boxes are filled with diverse arrangements of thick ply strips and long wood screws. All of these I will explain.

Naturally enough, furniture varies more than guitars do. The hand tools needed to make a guitar are not many, and some the competent woodworker may well choose to make for himself. All of these are described in this book and there are a few detailed which the enthusiast may choose to buy if they are not in his cabinet-maker's armoury.

THE GUITAR

The guitar is a complex arrangement: an example of the whole being more than the sum of its parts. It must be strong because it has something like 35kg of string tension stress on it constantly although it may weigh only 1.5kg. It must, of course, be light enough to vibrate, but not everywhere the same. Some parts are the stable background against which such vibrations work if they are not simply to be dissipated and lost before their time. It must spread its different frequencies of vibration into areas of wood designed to give them equal voice with a suitable compromise between harmony and separation. This must all be contained within the confines of the traditional shape and styling of the Spanish original. Although there are some who would depart from the traditional styling in search of some specific variation of performance, nevertheless the highest quality hand-built guitars do achieve the best of standards within the tradition. The achievement of the highest standards of sound quality in the guitars of the best master luthiers is a balance of craft, creative art and intuitive 'feel' which I cannot explain.

8

Thin ply templates and guards
in a bewildering array.

The alignment of parts demands extreme accuracy and subtlety if the player is to express himself through the instrument with clarity and sensitivity but no excess effort. Strings must vibrate easily without touching other parts and yet must be as close to the fingerboard as compromise will allow for ease of playing. Just as important to some players, the visual embellishments must be harmoniously designed and near perfectly executed without any compromise to the other qualities.

All this may begin to sound like a rather extreme demand in a material as organic and variable as wood. So it is, but it is not impossible and it is something which can be worked steadily towards. There are ways of perfecting the skills necessary to make a guitar which will almost certainly exceed the performance of the laminated student factory models seen in high-street music shops. I shall do my best to lead you through the methods and around the pitfalls that are bound to surround the first time guitar maker.

I still have my first guitar as my own performance instrument. It reminds me of its imperfections still but to one who had played one of the better factory models for years with satisfaction, it was an absolute revelation. I do hope that yours, if you choose to start, will challenge and enlarge you in your woodworking and challenge and reward you in your playing. I hope that it will then further challenge you to find out how much better your second guitar could be.

LEVELS OF SKILL

I am aware that it will be difficult to lead the beginner at guitar making through the highly skilled work of the luthier without explaining what may to some seem obvious and without leaving others to make potentially expensive mistakes. I intend to explain all the processes I use and how I achieve them. If you are knowledgeable enough about your own techniques and approach, vary the methods suggested by all means but with caution and only with good reason. Clearly I have significantly changed and developed the methods that I have read about, otherwise this book would simply be a rehash of previous literature on the subject. I am confident that it is not.

I came to luthiery after a period of cabinet-making which had challenged my woodworking skills continually. As part of this, and also quite separately, I have had experience of turning. I have most particularly enjoyed marquetry. If I were to suggest that you take the same route to hone your skills to the required level then your first guitar would be a very long way off. So to a considerable extent I am expecting you, the reader, to be capable of doing what I can do. In many cases I will explain some materials and methods that you can practise on. For example, it is possible to buy from Luthier's Supplies reject front timber. It is not good for making a guitar but you can certainly practise front techniques on it if you are not confident of cutting straight into your first good piece. Joinery softwood, some of which is essential anyway,

can be used to practise such things as heel carving and head drilling and slotting.

I will not explain how to sharpen standard tools. I will expect that the reader has learned how to get the optimum performance from planes, chisels, carving tools and saws. The cabinet scraper in particular is an invaluable tool. Perfectly set up it cuts like a magic laser beam but for me to explain its sharpening would duplicate existing literature. I do recommend that the reader search out sharpening techniques in the literature as all the methods explained do rely on optimally sharpened and set tools.

The reader may notice that the photo illustrations show older-style wooden tooling whereas modern tools are of metal construction. This is just an idiosyncrasy of mine; you may use any tools you have. The more observant might also notice a complete lack of watch or jewellery about the hands. This I do recommend as working practice. Any hard materials can mark the soft front timbers you are going to work and should be avoided. It's bad enough having fingernails!

The life of a working luthier – plastic armadillos, electric cricket bats – they all need repair.

2 The Tools

Clearly many woodwork processes can be achieved in a variety of ways depending on the tools available. The most efficient tool to do a job could be decided upon by the speed with which it can complete the task. This is only one view of efficiency and it is the approach of the professional wood machinist. If you want to learn how to do an exacting new task then the best tool becomes the easiest one to control – sometimes the slowest in fact. To learn a new technique it is best to work at a speed which gives you plenty of time to think what you are doing and how well it is going. So, in general, I shall recommend hand-tool methods for making your first guitar. The principal exception, I suppose, is the almost ubiquitous electric drill. Once you have gained confidence and a competent view of what you are trying to achieve, machine tooling can be brought in to speed the work as you go on to make further instruments.

WORK-BENCH AND WORK-BOARDS

Your work-bench must be sturdy enough to withstand heavy planing. Also at some stages it is very valuable to be able to move around at least three sides of it. You will need a good vice, firmly fitted. This bench is quite probably your old friend and campaigner but it is very likely to show the marks of previous 'campaigns'. The first thing I am going to suggest is that you make it at least one new false top.

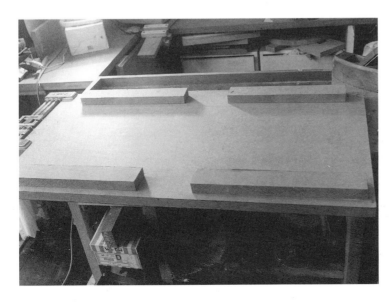

A 60 × 95cm work-board with locating battens.

11

A WORK-BOARD

MDF (25mm thickness at least) has a particularly fine smooth surface which is ideal. The 'work-board' should be at least 50cm wide and longer than this (mine is 60 × 95cm). It must overhang the front edge of your work-bench by about 10cm. It is located on the bench top by a series of battens on its underside which you will have to design for yourself to fit your own bench. It must lift on and off readily and when fitted it must not move about. It must be possible to fit a G-cramp on the opposite side, cramping the board down to the bench to allow you to apply your weight to the front overhang.

CHISELS

In addition to a couple of ordinary chisels, some specialist carving chisels are very useful. I use a large carver's skew and a couple of widths of dog-leg chisels (details given in relevant chapters). You cannot really do without at least one very narrow chisel for clearing purfling channels. I use two: 1mm and 1.5mm.

SAWS

An additional gent's saw is needed, purpose bought or modified for fretting (*see* Chapter 12).

ABRASIVES

Abrasive sheets have come a long way since sandpaper! I am phasing out all paper-backed abrasives from the workshop as being out of date. I suggest that you investigate the fabric-backed abrasives which are now available. The coarse and medium grades of these are aimed initially at the wood-turner and the finer grades derive from the aerospace industry. All can be washed and reused many times.

Whether you use the coarsest grades may depend on your liking for rasps and files as shaping tools. Something like 60 or 80 grit abrasive cloth makes a very good alternative to these. For wood finishing you will probably need 120, 180, 240, 320 and 400. For working on the lacquer surfaces, the range of 'micromesh' abrasives start at 1500 and go on to 1800, 2400, 3200 and further.

For maximum control and longevity, cloth-backed abrasives can be contact

The tramelling inlay cutter and marker.

A TRAMMELLING INLAY CUTTER

This should be made from a hard and dense timber. It is designed to hold a variety of cutting blades in a sliding bar; a pencil can also be fitted. It is intended as a universal tool to cut or mark circles or to cut one or two incisions any distance in from a curved surface, i.e. guitar outline, or from a straight-edged piece. It adjusts very positively with a screwdriver.

I used a dark rosewood spindle turning blank which proved ideal. Using a 50 × 50mm piece, I cut a section 90mm long for the body and one 150mm long for the cutter bar. Brass strip is readily available in good modeller's shops.

The body of the tool needs a 15mm square mortise 12mm from one end and central to its width. The best way to achieve this is to mark this in both sides and then to cut the body down through one side of the mortise so that it can be cut out as a housing joint with saw and chisel. Cut a piece out from the body so that the mortise in the moving bar will come to lie flush with the body surface when pushed in as far as possible. This allows the blade to be set on zero cut width.

After drilling and cutting a hexagonal hole for the nut the body can be glued back together. Ensure that the bar will still slide in the body. The end of the body can now be drilled centrally to allow a piece of brass rod or dowel to be fitted as a trammel pivot with epoxy. The width is optional. Mine is 9mm dowel extending 12mm from the body underside. The bar should be able to be fitted from either side and either way up.

One face of the body must now be marked and planed into a circle in such a way that the cutter can be made to follow an inside curve of approximately 2.5cm radius.

A pencil can be fitted and held; no. 11 scalpel blades can be held and cutters can be made from old jigsaw blades. These should be rubbed down on a grindstone or a coarse sharpening stone to give an obtuse angled point which is sharpened like a chisel, i.e. with one dead flat side.

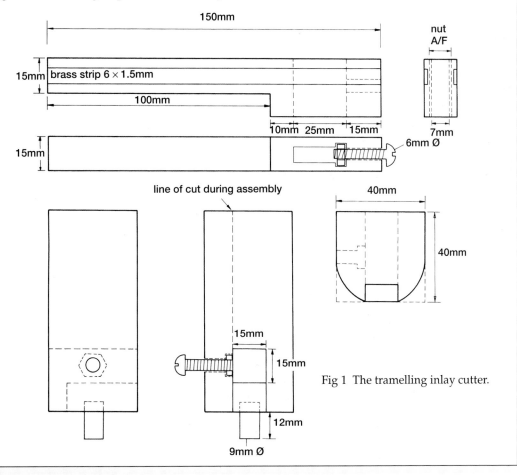

Fig 1 The tramelling inlay cutter.

glued on to flat or curved surfaces to make your own rasps, emery boards and so on. You will find it particularly useful to obtain a range of wooden cylinders such as dowels and broom handles and set up sanding rods with one grade each end. Do a range of flat ones, too.

GLUES

There are so many adhesives on the woodworking market today that confusion has often kept pace with the technical terminology. Fortunately, only a few relatively well-established types are of use to the luthier.

In the body of the guitar it is necessary that the adhesive dries brittle-hard. Only this kind of bond will efficiently transfer vibrations from one piece of timber to the next. It is also important that the glue does not stain timber surfaces in any way. In the event of repair work being necessary the guitar (at least its back edge joint) can be disassembled with heat and/or a little water. These constraints mean that there are only two suitable adhesives. The first is traditional animal glue, available in brown pearls and made up in heated water. The use of this is well covered in older cabinet-making literature. The vast majority of luthiers use a ready-made double-cream-consistency emulsion which is classed as an Aliphatic Resin and goes by the name of Titebond. This dries by loss of its water phase and not by cooling. It has to be borne in mind in some situations that you are wetting the surfaces to be glued but I shall cover this point at the appropriate time.

After trying several types of glue gun I am now convinced that a large (probably veterinary-sized) syringe is the best way to dispense Titebond.

Not to be confused with titebond is PVA. This is a much whiter, slower-drying emulsion and dries to a relatively soft clear plastic consistency. It can be used for some of the associated carpentry, i.e. the mould, but is never used on the guitar.

Epoxy-resin adhesives contain no water but they also set to a softer material. Since they set rather than drying they do not have any tendency to shrink so an epoxy glue line is likely to remain visible where a titebond line would shrink and disappear, further assisting the close adherence of the timber members. Nevertheless, epoxies are of some use if you wish to mount neck reinforcements and I shall describe one of their applications in the chapter on Finishing.

Cyano-acrylates can also have their uses. The liquid types are too thin but gel types with accelerator liquids can speed the mounting of binding strips on the edge of the instrument as I shall explain.

I have found no use for any of the 'powder mixed with water' types.

STICKY TAPES

Again, there are very many such adhesive tapes on the market and I shall mention at least three.

Clear cellulose tapes can often prove too sticky and may tear surface fibres particularly out of soft frontwood. They can be very variable in tensile strength and are best avoided.

The brown plastic parcel tapes have their uses. They can provide a useful quick barrier against the accidental adherence of glues and their greater strength and slight elasticity can be used in drawing parts together while glue sets. Like the clear types, they should not be applied to the guitar front.

'Masking' tapes are very useful and, after checking on scrap pieces, can generally be used if necessary on the front. They are also necessary for masking the fingerboard before finishing. More than one width will prove useful.

'Low tack' sheet is used in fitting the bridge. This is a bit like book-covering plastic sheet but much less sticky. It is used, in more than one grade, by engravers. You may be able to purchase a length from your local trophy engraver.

LIGHTING

There is no doubt that the very best kind of light to work by is natural daylight. However, direct sunlight may damage some timbers so care must be taken in arranging your workbench with respect to windows. Work by bright indirect daylight if you can but I would encourage you

to think of lighting as a form of tooling. Control of light direction can only be done with well-designed lighting equipment. A controllable swivel lamp is a good idea, fixed on or adjacent to the work-bench. Ceiling-mounted lighting is useful especially when applying or polishing finish lacquer. Clip-on spotlights are cheap and convenient and I recommend them as workshop tools.

CRAMPS

In many applications associated with instruments, G-cramps are too heavy for the thin timbers and lightweight constructions. With no joints to hold timbers while gluing they are inclined to slide on their glue layer especially with the weight of a metal cramp offset to one side. I have made up several arrangements which use wooden or ply strips and ordinary wood

Think of lighting equipment as tools. Lighting direction can be critical.

To Make …

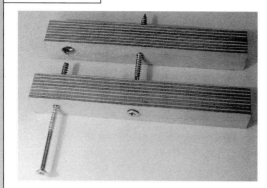

LIGHTWEIGHT SCREWCRAMPS

The old-style woodworker's hand screw vice is the original from which I have conceived my screwcramp. It uses two wooden strips, two large wood screws and one very small one with a cup washer. It provides a strong lightweight cramp with less tendency to allow side-slip. Several sizes will be needed but these are very quick to make and cost little.

(*Left*) A light and simple cramp based on the old handscrew vice.

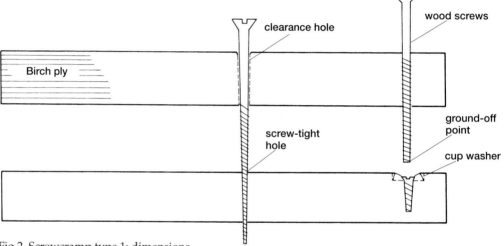

Fig 2 Screwcramp type 1: dimensions arbitrary, several sizes needed.

Extending this idea, I made cramps originally for fitting fingerboards that have come in handy for other jobs as well. Simple strips of thick ply with a hole at each end can be forced together with large woodscrews. They can be made to hold balsa-wood pads to protect soft timbers.

Fingerboard cramp.

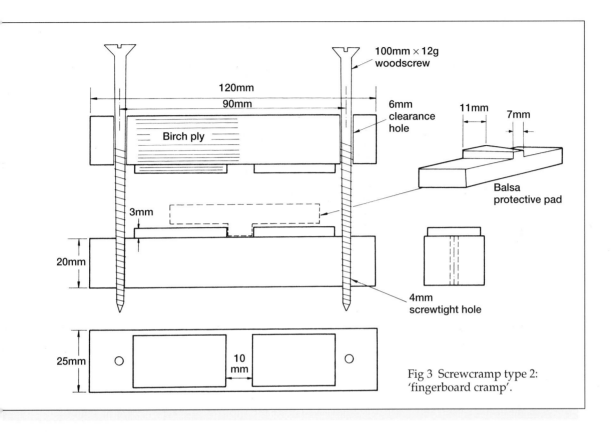

Fig 3 Screwcramp type 2: 'fingerboard cramp'.

screws. The simplest of these are strips of softwood with a screw through a clearance hole in the middle. These are dealt with in the assembly framework chapter.

PEGS

Pegs need to have a strong multicoil spring and can be used as cramps for the side linings. I keep about a hundred. Just occasionally one or two of them may not quite provide enough force and a woodscrew can be used to reinforce them. Drill one tight hole and one clearance hole and insert a flat-headed screw (countersunk screws split the pegs). A handful of these in your peg box can be very useful.

BUBBLE PLASTIC

Available from horticultural suppliers, this is the best protection for the softer timbers when on the work-bench. Harder fragments which would indent the front on any other surface will not do so on this. It is easy to wipe clean and will not hold particles on its surface as fabric does. Use it all the time when handling the assembled instrument.

PAPER

Wallpaper lining paper is cheap and conveniently rolled. Use it as bench protection for the front before assembly.

Essential tools. The guitar can be made with no more tools than these.

Very useful additional tooling.

3 Timbers

Each component part of a guitar has a different role to play and needs to be made of an appropriate material. If we were designing the guitar as a new invention of today we would probably make some of its components from synthetic materials. Carbon fibre has already found its way into some classical guitars and, in the early 50s Mario Maccaferri made perfectly playable guitars largely of plastics. The traditional classical guitar, however, is made almost entirely of four or five timber species, each carefully chosen.

THE FRONT

The front or soundboard of a guitar is almost invariably made of softwood. The term 'softwood', of course, denotes wood of a cone-bearing tree and has little to do with hardness, but chosen timbers are usually quite soft and consequently need care in handling.

The best wood is from trees which have grown slowly so that their annual rings are close together. They have grown close amid other trees so that they have developed straight and their lower branches have died off quickly. Only from trees grown in forests in a cold climate and/or high altitude can we hope to get half-metre lengths of straight, knot-free timber where 20cm of radial growth has annual rings which tell of the lifetimes of several generations of luthiers.

The timber is first split on natural cleavage planes and then cut radially into pairs of sheets so that fibres run nearly parallel to the surfaces and the layers of harder latewood run at right angles to the surface but straight along the piece. These skills are provided to most of us by our luthier's supplier.

The very best front material consists of two adjacent sheets of wood approximately 500mm × 200mm × 4–5mm. They should show an almost perfect mirror image of grain pattern. They will have lighter early wood layers and darker late wood layers running as straight as a ruler at not much more than 1mm intervals. They should be so accurately radial that they show marks running across the main grain pattern where the very tiny radially arranged wood fibres (medullary rays) lie across the surface. Flexed across the grain it should feel remarkably stiff for its weight and thickness. Picked up by the centre of one long side and knuckle tapped just off centre it should sound like a distant bell. What I am describing is the perfect front blank. It is the product of a remarkable train of events of growth, selection and skilled dissection. Not surprisingly then, it is expensive. For your early work in guitar making something less perfect will be more appropriate. Nevertheless it is by the criteria mentioned above that one tests a potential piece of wood for a front: if it sounds as if it will 'ring' and the appearance is acceptable.

King among such timbers is European Spruce, a very pale timber with a rather faint medullary ray system. Also very good is Western Red Cedar, usually from North America and a much darker red-brown

European Spruce (lightest), W.R. Cedar (darkest) and Sitka.

colour. American Spruce is usually Sitka Spruce. This is a straw-coloured timber with a much more marked system of radial growth resulting sometimes in an interesting almost chequerboard pattern on the surface. Other timbers are sometimes available, such as Silver Fir, Yellow Cedar, Engelmann Spruce and others. Reputable suppliers will only sell suitable species. Listing all such species and attempting to distinguish them is beyond the scope of this book.

THE BACK AND SIDES

The back and sides are also bought as prepared blanks by the vast majority of luthiers. The back will be two adjacent sheets of the same size as described above for the front. Matching them as far as possible for grain and colour the sides will probably have been cut from another piece as these need to be 800mm × 120mm × 3–4mm

again as two adjacent leaves of timber. Generally the timber will be cut radially as described for the front but some timbers show more interesting grain figure if cut tangentially. So, for example, a sample of flamed grain Maple will be cut radially to give the best figure while Maple with bird's eye figure will be cut tangentially, otherwise its particular features would be lost.

Specifying the type is more difficult. Softwoods can be used: Cypress is the traditional timber for the flamenco guitar and Yew can be used to good effect but most classical guitars are made with hardwood back and sides. The most prized and sought-after timber is Rio Rosewood. Good Rio Rosewood is a remarkable timber in both appearance and its almost metallic bell-like sound when tapped but it is now virtually all gone. When it is available it is usually of poor quality and high price. A near relative of Rio Rosewood, and regularly used for the best guitars, is Indian Rosewood. It is not as hard or dense nor as interestingly colour varied. It is a dark purple brown and acoustically ideal but not particularly cheap.

Also very good and probably underrated acoustically is Mahogany. This is so much softer and lighter that it is seems improbable that it could do any job for which a rosewood might be specified. It is also a much lighter and plainer colour and, while not unattractive it is not striking. Good Mahogany comes from Brazil and Honduras and is, of course, under environmental pressure.

The Acer group – Maple and Sycamore provide a range of acoustically good timber types. While a few years ago it might have been unfortunately stained red-brown, blonde-backed guitars now seem to be increasing in popularity and the appearance of flame or bird's eye can be most striking.

Left to right: Imbuya, bird's eye
Maple, Rosewood, flamed Maple
and (unfinished) Walnut.

Highly figured Acers can be tricky to plane. Plain Maple can be one of the easiest timbers to work and is beginning to replace hard-to-get Cypress on flamenco guitars. Torres didn't despise the Maple so why should we?

There are many other timbers available and I offer my thoughts on some I have tried. Wenge is acoustically excellent. It is one of those densely hard timbers with the same sort of 'metal sheet' ring that Rio Rosewood has. However, it is very hard and tricky to plane, it will skewer you with splinters like a porcupine and it is very open grained when it comes to finishing. Make a guitar with it one day, but not your first. As striking in its own way as Rio Rosewood is Cocobolo, a timber of dark striped red. It has the kind of hard, dense structure which makes for good acoustics but hard woodwork. Walnut seems to have much in common with plain Maple as being acoustically good and reasonably easy to work. Figured samples make very attractive guitars but I recommend plain samples for your first efforts. Imbuya is also known as

Brazilian Walnut, not for any botanical reason but perhaps for general colouring. It can come with some strange blotchy appearances but it works well. Ovangkol is a darkish hard timber with something of a Satinwood-type grain pattern at times. This doesn't improve its ease of planing but it is not the worst and it can be quite striking of appearance once finished.

THE NECK

The tension on a set of guitar strings is approximately 35kg. These pull at a very slight angle on the neck (and its supporting fingerboard). This pull could, over a considerable period of time, cause a warping of the neck forward, raising the action and destroying the accuracy of intonation. Neck timbers need to be permanently resistant to this sideways stress all in a half oval cross-section no more than 15mm × 50mm. It must also be light in density to maintain the balance of the instrument.

21

In addition, and more difficult to define, the neck needs to be able to hold half the length of the strings without losing any of the energy that they are putting into the soundboard of the instrument. Some timbers, while seeming structurally good, produce a slightly muted sound in the finished instrument.

Two timbers have come to occupy a dominant position in their suitability for neck timber: Mahogany and Cedrela (Cedar). Mahogany has already been mentioned. Cedrela is a hardwood timber from Central America. Its relationship to the softwood Cedar is in terms of smell (its Latin name is *Cedrela odorata*). It resembles Mahogany but is lighter in colour and in weight.

Other timbers have been used. The chapter on neck construction considers how the arrangement of timbers may overcome some of their inadequacies. I have used Beech, and I have even seen Elm used apparently effectively, but opinion over the years of guitar making have been unanimous and there are only really two timbers on the list.

THE FINGERBOARD

The fingerboard assists the neck in doing its job but also has its own structural requirements. Fingerboards need to be made of a material sufficiently hard to resist the wear of left-hand nails and the strings that are pushed down on them. They need to cut sufficiently accurately to produce a good fret slot and they must grip the tang of the fret.

Ebony has become the standard for fingerboards of high-quality guitars. It is hard and dense with a smooth and even grain and many people feel that the stark black shows off well-polished frets to give the best overall appearance. However, it may take over a year to stop drying and shrinking. If it shrinks further after being attached to the neck and fretted, it can either split down the middle or produce a problem with fret ends.

Less dense timbers season more readily and are in some ways easier to work. There are those who feel that timbers with a more defined grain structure than the flat matt black of Ebony actually look more attractive. Most suppliers will also list Indian Rosewood as fingerboard blanks and this is less likely to cause the problems that Ebony will over a short time span.

Many other timbers are perfectly suitable for your first fingerboard. Anything over 450mm long × 70mm square can be cut up into 8mm strips for fingerboards. In this way I have used Bubinga, Sonokeling, Utile and Pau Rosa turning blanks. If you don't have a bandsaw, I recommend Indian Rosewood from your luthier's supplies.

STRUTTING

The soundboard of a guitar requires a system of reinforcing and vibration-dispersing structures on its inside. The accepted wisdom seems to be that this should be made of the same material as the front itself. Sections of edge scrap from the front are probably not thick enough for fan struts. In any case, they won't provide the two cross braces that are needed. What you need is a sample of softwood of straight close grain which is light in weight. I recommend that you try your local joinery timber stockist for pieces of 12mm × 25mm planed pine. This size tends to be made from knot-free straight-grained stuff which is cheap and often ideal. Another perhaps unlikely source is the mouldings section at your DIY store.

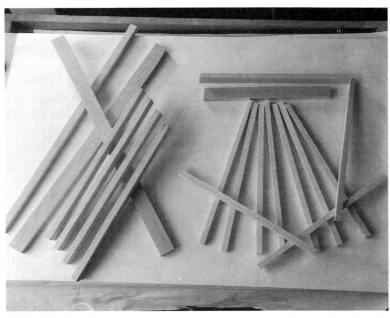

(Above) Joinery 12 × 25mm with grain in best direction.

Luthier's Supplies' packs for making steel-string (L) and classical (R) strutting.

If all else fails, Luthier's Supplies will provide you with timber to make strutting and cross-bracing sections.

LININGS

The linings of a guitar are intended to increase the gluing surface area between the front and sides and the back and sides. There are several ways to produce these and attach them to the curved inner contour of the instrument. The method used will influence the nature of the timber; I shall go on to explain a very easy method which uses modeller's ply. Soft and relatively flexible timbers such as Willow and Lime are often recommended. The spare timber of which the sides are made can be utilized. If you opt for cutting kerfed linings then, again, I can recommend suitably selected 12mm × 25mm joinery pine.

BINDINGS AND PURFLING

The bindings of the guitar are the edge strips which protect the curved corners of the front and back of the body and may provide decorative colour contrast. The purfling strips are the decorative inlay strips between binding and front or back. They may be included between front and binding and/or between side and binding and they may be used to decorate elsewhere. These pieces of wood need to be sufficiently flexible to be pushed into their positions without breaking or to be heat bent in the same way as the sides. Bindings are often 2mm thick and it may well be necessary to heat bend them to the waist. Front edge purflings usually present no problem but side purfling strips can be quite tricky to fit unless they will heat bend with an iron as suggested in the chapter on Inlaying Work. Timbers used for decoration need to be close grained and

23

non-porous, otherwise when sanding, dust from other coloured timbers can leave them looking scruffy. If you were to use a porous timber like Ash adjacent to something like Ebony it would make a bit of a mess at the final sanding stage. Pre-prepared purfling from reputable suppliers will be suitable. I do go on to suggest ways of making your own designs of purfling.

Some attractively coloured timber strips, can shed their colours into the finishing material you use and cause colour runs into adjacent woods. Check by rubbing them with the lacquer solvent on a white cloth. I have found Padauk strips seductively attractive but they bleed pink into paler timbers with my finishing techniques.

MODELLER'S PLY

This material is invaluable in the making of protective masks and templates at many stages of the work on a guitar. Modeller's supplies normally stock several thicknesses.

The most useful is 1.5mm. This can be bought in small sizes but is most economical if you buy sheets of 5ft sq. Such sheets roll up into quite a tight cylinder for carrying. The material cuts easily with good scissors or a craft knife and I shall go on to describe many ways in which it is used in guitar making.

HUMIDITY AND TIMBER

All timbers react to their surroundings, taking up or losing moisture. As they take up water they swell and as they lose it they shrink. These dimensional changes are greatest tangentially and are least in terms of the length of the timber. Since a guitar contains more than one timber and, in places, timbers are glued long grain to cross grain (think of the bridge glued across the front) it is not possible to construct a guitar which can avoid internal stresses as ambient temperature/humidity changes take place. The best that can be

Binding (Ebony) and purflings in a Rosewood/Spruce guitar.

Weighing machine, dehumidifier and drying rack with enough for about 25 instruments and purfling storage.

done is to ensure that, at the point of assembly, all the timbers are in equilibrium with air in normal housing. As many international performers have found to their cost, taking a guitar in and out of a wide range of temperature/humidity changes can damage it to a greater or lesser extent.

Humidity affects both the timescale over which a first guitar can be constructed and the locations suitable as a workshop. My own response to this is to maintain the air in my centrally heated workshop at a relative humidity of 45 per cent by means of an electric dehumidifier and to keep it controlled by observation of a hygrometer. Hygrometers with a dial are available and dehumidifiers are now common in electrical shops.

There is no point maintaining this RH at the expense of electricity if the timber is used before it has acclimatized itself to the workshop air. The only convenient and completely accurate way of assessing this seems to me to be weight. I am fortunate in having a simple laboratory balance which enables me to weigh pieces below 1kg to the nearest gram.

Every piece of timber that I buy has its date and weight written on it and is reweighed at intervals. This shows when it has stopped losing weight and is thus, presumably, acclimatized, although weight loss does become very slow towards the end point. I have never bought timber from any supplier which has failed to lose weight so I am content that this effort is not wasted.

25

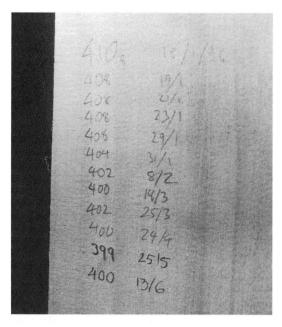

Weighing records clearly marked on each blank.

I find that softwood blanks for guitar fronts tend to take three months or so to acclimatize but hardwood blanks for the backs and sides take longer despite their similar thickness. Neck blanks can take up to six months but Ebony for fingerboards can still be losing weight fifteen months or more after purchase. Rosewood fingerboard thicknesses take about a third of this. These times are naturally generalizations and depend partly on the conditions at the supplier's stores. I recommend that you visit and buy your first batch of timbers in person and take some note of storage conditions.

Having bought your timber you should not start too soon nor store the timbers in a draughty outdoor shed or garage. If there is no choice as to workspace, perhaps the parts can be brought indoors between operations.

Luthier's Supplies' beautiful rosettes. One of these will usually be needed.

4 The Assembly Framework

THE MOULD

The technique explained in this book relies on a softwood framework and template called 'the Mould'. It acts as a template in marking out the timbers for the front and back of the instrument. It is used as a shape template in bending the sides and it can help correct any minor errors of symmetry at this stage. It also obviates the need to buy or construct a multitude of cramps. Simple strips of softwood and screws fitted around the perimeter of the mould provide all the cramping force necessary during assembly. There is no need for it to be highly finished or polished, but care must be taken that it is fairly accurately symmetrical, that it is flat and that the inside surfaces are at right angles to the front face.

This mould is made up as a composite block of 75mm × 75mm planed square joinery softwood. Good-quality stock must be obtained and acclimatized in the workshop. Large knots and splits should be avoided. This should not be too difficult as much of the softwood is cut into short sections. The outline plan of the guitar needs to be drawn on paper and on stiff card or modeller's plywood before work commences. (For shape(s) *see* Chapter 16.)

Sections of the square stock are cut and assembled overlapping the paper outline. Dimensions are somewhat arbitrary but suggestions are given in diagram form. The longer lengths at the centre line allow screws to attach the two halves. The individual blocks are PVA glued and cramped to their adjacent blocks (NB not on the

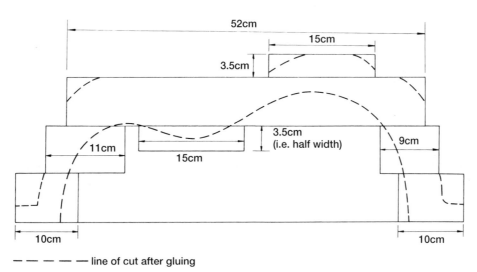

Fig 4 Suggested cutting diagram for mould.

Sections are cut and assembled overlapping the outline.

(*Below*) The ends are screwed together and an outline drawn on both faces.

centre line) until each half is a stepped block overlapping the outline completely.

The extended blocks on the centre line are cut away and drilled (2.5mm) to allow 75mm no. 8 screws to hold the halves together. Widen the hole to 4mm on the screw head half. Screw the two halves firmly together, then nominate the best face as the front and plane it true and flat as necessary. With the front face down on a flat surface lay your stiff plan outline of the guitar on top to cover the central space completely with its centre line accurately on the mould centre join and draw around it. If you have a band-saw it should be straightforward to cut around this outline on both halves and reassemble to finish the mould.

If you are using hand tools you will need to separate the two halves, project the centre line points to the front face of the mould with a set square and reassemble to redraw the outline on the front face, hopefully in perfect register with the copy on the back face. With a hand saw make numerous cuts in each half that just touch the lines on the front and back surfaces, and remove wastes with a chisel. Some gouging or rasping may be needed to smooth the surface to the lines front and rear. Right angles with the front face must be maintained all round the outline.

Ensure symmetry by placing the halves on top of each other and cutting as necessary. A little overcutting can be corrected with paste or body fillers without detriment.

This mould will allow us to mark the instrument outline as necessary and acts as a template when bending the sides. It can then hold the sides in shape to prevent them restraightening, which they sometimes tend to do.

In this form it will not allow the neck in to join to the sides. If you opt for the dovetailed neck join this will not matter, but the traditional slipper joint needs an opened neck. With the mould in two halves drill, countersink and drive home two 75mm screws into each half of the upper bout framework and then remove them. With your widest chisel and a mallet, resting on a firm support, it is necessary to split the short grain alongside where the neck will

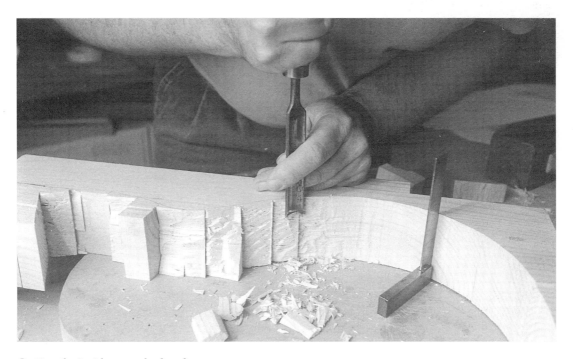

Cutting the inside curve by hand.

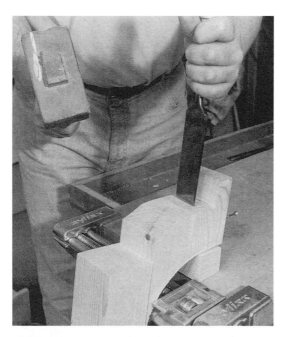

Splitting out the neck opening …

… ensures an accurate fit.

be approximately 35–40mm either side of the central joint. A neatly split off block should result which can immediately and accurately be replaced by reinserting the two screws. The split along the natural grain ensures correct register and effectively prevents incorrect reassembly.

With the two neck pieces removed the mould is held together only by two screws at the bottom and, with much shorter

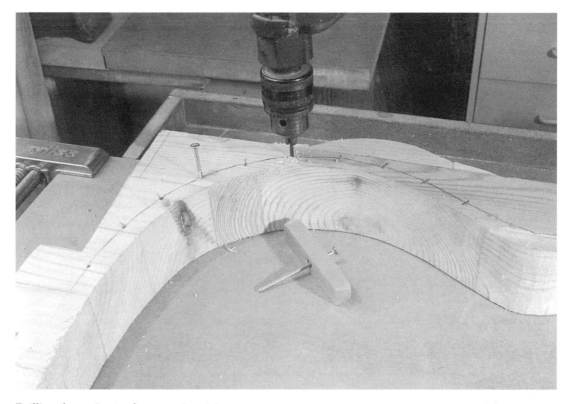

Drilling the perimeter for cramping strips.

grain timber, can be a bit fragile in this state. Plywood pieces cut to the outline of the mould and glued to the face side can be used as reinforcement but are optional.

On the back side of the mould mark a line about 12–15mm outside the outline. Mark off a point on this line every 40–50mm around the outline but not including the removable neck pieces. At each point drill a 3mm hole at least 50mm deep. Drive in a 75mm screw and remove. For each hole you will need a screw and a piece of softwood 100mm × 15mm × 15mm or similar section drilled centrally with a 4mm hole. These form the assembly cramps. The screws should drive in and come out firmly but without excessive resistance. If a screw

strips its thread, insert a 2mm strip of glue-smeared veneer.

THE BACKBOARD

You need a substantial rigid ply, blockboard or MDF sheet, e.g. 25mm thick. It needs to be 100mm wider than your mould and about 300mm longer. Draw a centre line along its length and place the mould on it in correct alignment. Ensure that the top inner edge of the mould where the neck will go is less than half the string length (usually 325mm) from that edge of the board so that the head with its face veneers clears the board. Clamp the mould in this position.

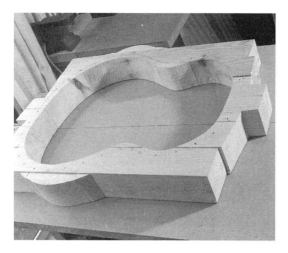

The mould on its backboard.

Drill through from the rear of the board into substantial parts of the mould and fix it on with 75mm screws, countersunk and driven firmly home. Check the centre alignment.

To align the neck a series of lines can be drawn parallel to the centre line each side and numbered clearly or colour coded. Alternatively, this can be done by sticking on graph or squared paper.

In the next chapter reasons are given why it is recommended to build a guitar with a domed front. The flat inner part of the mould therefore needs to be removed. Mark a line 15mm in from the edge of the mould all round the inside of the guitar shape and remove the mould. With a jigsaw or keyhole saw remove this central area so that when the mould is replaced there is a 15mm ledge all around the inside.

The edge of this cut needs to be slightly rounded and softened with a chisel and abrasives so that no hard line of the edge can mark the soft instrument front timber that is going to be firmly pressed against it. Finally, varnish or seal the mould bottom inside edge and the ledge on its inside against the accidental adherence of glue. Smooth off with a finer abrasive once the varnish is hardened.

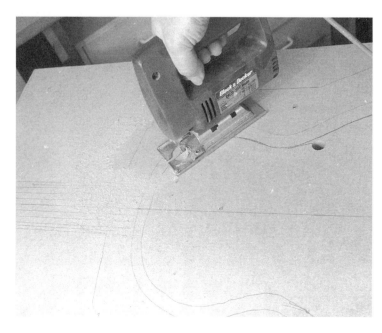

The inner part of the backboard needs to be removed.

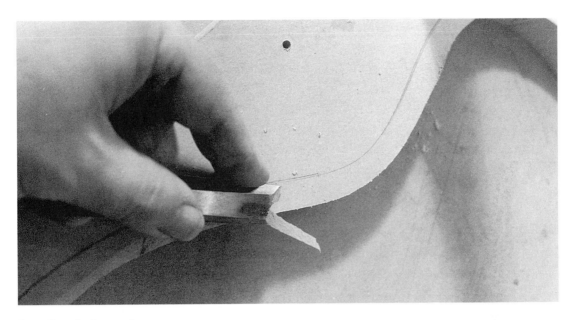

Rounding the inner edge.

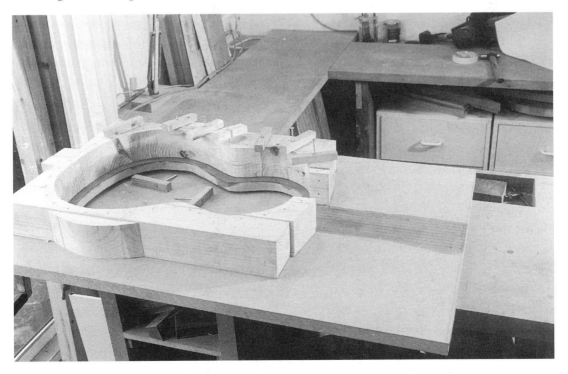

The finished mould. Note the neck alignment marks are varnished to prevent rubbing off. The backboard edge will hold the mould vertical in a vice. Cut it off flush if you want it to stand on edge.

5 The Front

JOINTING

Having obtained a suitable front blank, you have two pieces of wood which you need to match up into their original position in the tree. Good suppliers will usually place crayon marks across one edge to show this. If not, you need to look at external marks to work out which faces match best. Usually the grain lines will be closer together down one side of the piece. The wider-spaced grain lines represent the inner part of the trunk which were part of a young tree. As the tree grows its grain lines become closer together. Open out the two leaves so that the closest grain lines meet in the middle and place these edges together. If these close grain lines are not parallel to the edge

you will need to mark a ruler line very lightly along the straightest grain line you can find near to the edge. This should be cut down carefully with a sharp craft knife. If the grain is not very near to dead straight you will need a straight edge. Place the two pieces back together in register and cut along the identical grain line of the other piece. With a well cut front blank this procedure should be unnecessary.

In order to glue the two pieces together along the centre line of the front it is necessary to have two perfectly matching flat edges which will be in contact over the whole length. This is the job of a jointing or trying plane which is usually 550mm long; just about the length of a typical front blank. You will need a piece of timber at

Jointing the front.

least 500mm long and thick enough to raise the two softwood pieces to near the centre of the sole of your long plane lying on its side. Holding or cramping the softwood sheets on this piece you can run the long plane on its side, along the surfaces to be jointed. Once a pair of shavings is being taken off the whole length, reset the plane to take a thinner shaving. If you take one piece in each hand and offer up the mating surfaces to each other they should be in total contact. There should not be a point in the middle about which the ends can be pivoted neither should it be possible to flex them to separate a point in the middle while the ends remain in contact. There must be friction contact all the way along.

Held up to the light, it should not be possible to see any hairlines of light between the surfaces to be joined.

If you do not have a 550mm, plane do this with the longest plane that you do have. An alternative which some people use is a straight edge with abrasive sheeting contact adhered over a 500mm length. A good spirit level can be used in this way. If it is necessary to use a piece of thick ply or MDF for this they must be accurately flat and they will have to have abrasive sheet adhered to both sides or they will not remain sufficiently accurate.

The two sheets must be glued together with Titebond while being lightly pressed together and held down flat. There are several ways of achieving light pressure. One is to cramp battens of wood alongside the pieces on the workboard so that they can be braced in opposed pairs with wooden wedges. This can depend on the outer edge being fairly straight. It can also be done with brown elastic parcel tape stretched across and pressed down firmly both across the face of the pieces

Using the elasticity of parcel tape …

… to hold the joint together and flat.

and on to the work-board surface. Whichever is used, it is always advisable to run a length of tape along the work-board centre line to prevent the adhesion of glue. It may well be necessary to place weights at some points along the join to ensure that it does not have a step when it dries. Cover the underside of all such weights with brown parcel tape, as wooden weights will otherwise adhere and metal weights can stain. Once dried it should be possible to hold it by one long edge and tap a clear, buzz free tone from it. Buzzing may be caused by an unjoined piece of centre line.

If the face you have designated as the front is very rough it can be planed a little at this stage; otherwise this is best left till later. It needs to be smooth enough to allow accurate working with a craft knife. If your joint is really good it may be difficult to see so it should be picked out with a faint line from a 2B pencil.

Place the front, face up on the workboard and lay the mould over it, observing centre lines, into what seems the best position. Draw very lightly around the mould interior and remove. The next operation is to drill a hole at the centre point of the sound-hole and rosette.

CENTRE POINT OF THE SOUND-HOLE

The centre point of the guitar sound-hole and rosette depends on the scale length of your guitar (standard is 650mm) and the number of frets to be fitted as well as the diameter of the sound-hole which is planned. The diameter of the sound-hole will be influenced by the internal diameter of the rosette you plan to fit.

If you plan a 650mm scale length then fret 12, which always comes at the top margin of the body, is 325mm from the nut (top point of the fingerboard). Traditionally the sound-hole splits the nineteenth fret into two parts and the nineteenth fret comes 433mm from the nut. 433 minus 325 gives us 108. Subtracting 2mm from this to allow a space in the centre of the nineteenth fret gives 106mm from the top edge of the body to the edge of the hole. Measure the rosette internal diameter and subtract 4mm to arrive at

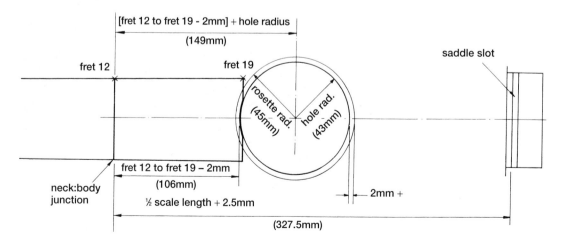

Fig 5 Layout of front features. Values in round brackets can vary.

the sound-hole diameter. Halve this to get the hole radius and add it on to the 106mm. So, if your rosette internal diameter is 90mm then $(90 - 4) \div 2 = 43$mm which, plus 106 gives 149mm from the top edge of the body to the hole centre. Your own particular circumstances must be taken into account if any parameter varies from those I have used as example. I recommend that you draw the whole thing out on paper full size to check.

(*Above*) Using a template to drill the hole.

Marking the sound-hole and rosette area.

So, having found the centre point of the sound-hole, mark it precisely and clearly with a pencil or a craft knife. Unfortunately, if you try to drill straight through this the hardness of the glue line will divert your drill point so I recommend that you make a template by drilling the correct-sized hole through a piece of ply at least 4mm thick. The hole must be the diameter of the dowel in the trammelling base of your inlay cutter. Drive three panel pins through the ply no more than 30mm from the hole so that their points protrude. Carefully position this to drill the hole accurately and press to locate the panel pins. Note that they will only puncture the top in the sound-hole scrap. Drill the hole for your trammelling base. You will also need to drill this diameter hole approximately 150mm from one end of your work-board just off-centre.

Lightly cramping your top at the end of the work-board with these two drilled holes in register, mount a pencil into your inlay cutter and lightly mark a circle the size of your sound-hole.

INLAYING THE ROSETTE

This must be carried out with no spaces or inaccuracies as these show up clearly. Also it cannot be assumed that your rosette is exactly circular as some are not. I recommend that you very lightly glue your rosette in place with five or six single spots of Titebond and place a weight on it until the glue is hard. The pencil line around the soundhole will guide in placing it correctly.

At this point you may decide whether you want pieces of the rosette to decorate the bridge with later on. At the level of the rosette your fingerboard will be just over 60mm wide. If you mark two lines 25mm from your centre line either side, these will mark off the endpieces of the rosette that you can cut off and use elsewhere. You will also need to make a caul to press down your rosette. This is a piece of 3 or 4mm ply about 1–2mm smaller all round than the rosette. Cover one side with brown parcel tape.

Taking a pointed scalpel with a new blade incise very carefully around both the inside and outside edge of your rosette.

Cutting the rosette in with a scalpel.

Lifting the rosette off with a palette knife.

Cutting the rosette channel edge.

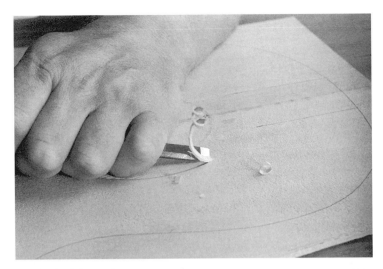

Rosette and caul ready – spare pieces removed.

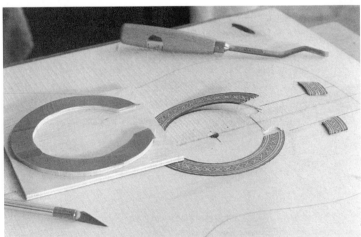

You will need to give thought to going round each quarter circle so that the harder latewood lines in the timber do not divert your knife away from the rosette. Once this is done all round, the rosette can be lifted off with a palette knife. With a very sharp chisel and great care you can start to cut away the channel you have incised the edge of. The rosette needs to be inlayed to a depth where planing the surface smooth will bring it level with the rosette. The plane will skim shavings off the top of the rosette but this should not occur before the surface is smooth. Your own rosette and the surface of your front blank must guide you here.

Once the inside edge of your channel is cut to a suitable depth, the centre part of the channel must be removed to this depth and a level bottom established. This is far from easy with ordinary chisels and the woodcarver's flat dogleg chisel is invaluable here. It may help to incise the waste in the channel with the inlay cutter.

Better still, if you have one, make the trammelling base for your router (*see* Chapter 16) and, after experimenting on a drilled piece of scrap, rout the channel bottom with a flat bottoming cutter. Avoid the scalpel-incised edges of the channel. Ensure that the bottom is flat and level and the inner corners are quite clean.

In gluing up to fit the rosette ensure that a little glue goes into the corner edges of the channel. You require some glue to squeeze up between the rosette and the front timber, most particularly on the inner side where all but 2mm of the front will be removed and there will be short grained timber which could fall out if it is not glued. Spread the glue, insert the rosette and press it in, looking for evidence of this glue around the edges. It will not be necessary to wipe small beads of glue away. Carefully place your rosette caul over the rosette and leave under a weight to dry.

PLANING

Once the rosette is in place you can start the all-important task of planing the front. It would be all right to plane the front 'in the square' but you are just as well to cut out most of its outline now. This can best be done with a fine sharp fret saw used over a supporting surface, ideally a fret saw table. A craft knife can be used with great care on a flat surface that you don't mind cutting into, but the risk of a split is greater. Cut away all but the top edge above the shoulders of the upper bout. This is useful for cramping purposes.

Your plane must be perfectly sharp and set up close mouthed and fine. If your blank is not perfectly straight to the grain, one side will plane 'against the grain' and irreparable damage could be done with an incautious stroke of a coarse-set plane. If this is the case, then cramp lightly at the bottom with a smooth caul such as a piece of hardboard and attempt to plane each half separately. NEVER plane toward your cramp or you may well smash the front beyond repair. In a bad case of a cross-grained front you will have to resort to grades of abrasives. This process is finished when the front and the rosette are smooth and level.

It is now necessary to place the front smooth-side down on a work-board. The surface you have so carefully planed is extremely soft and delicate and will be marked by contact with any particles such as wood fragments or glue drops. I recommend that every surface that you ever place the front down on is cleaned with the flat of your hand. A brush would remove loose particles only. Your hand will feel any particles that will not sweep off and they can be removed. Once cleaned and perfectly smooth, you can also cover the work-board with a sheet of clean paper such as wallpaper lining paper.

THICKNESSING

Planing the back surface smooth is not quite as critical as the front to begin with as more material has to be removed. Ultimately it becomes an extremely exacting task as the front of the guitar must be accurately thicknessed at all points. This is the operation most critical to the sound of the finished instrument.

Using the thickness gauge (described overleaf) frequently to check sizes I suggest that you plane down the front until the top bout is a constant thickness of 2.5mm down to the bottom end of the sound-hole. Allow this area to extend down approximately to

To Make …

A THICKNESS GAUGE

In order to check your progress you need a thicknessing gauge.

My suggested design for a simple thicknessing gauge is based on a sheet of 25mm birch ply which is very rigid. It could be built up from other materials. It needs an internal reach of 200mm.

Fig 6 Thickness gauge.

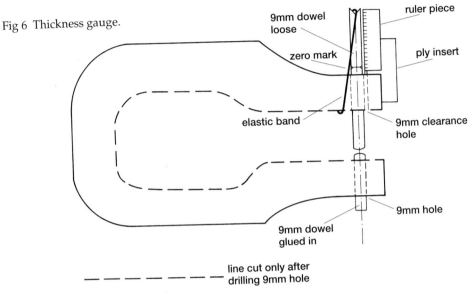

line cut only after
drilling 9mm hole

First, a long hole is drilled through the end the same diameter as a piece of dowel: the actual diameter of the dowel is not critical. It is then drilled halfway through with a close clearance hole. The interior is then cut out with fret or coping saw. Two suitable length pieces of dowel are then rounded at an end and one is glued into the tight-fitting hole. The other should drop through the clearance hole to meet it. A saw cut is made alongside the clearance hole and enlarged until a piece of 1.5mm ply is a firm fit in the slot. A piece of plastic ruler is cut and stuck on to this ply. An incision is made around the loose dowel to act as a zero mark. If possible, the rounding of the dowel ends and the incision are best done in a lathe. Moving the piece of ply with its ruler markings in the slot zeros the instrument against the incision mark on the loose dowel. Finally, a slot in the free dowel and a rubber band complete the assembly.

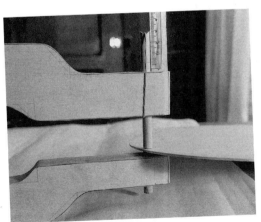

The thicknessing gauge in use.

Thicknessing the front.

the string end of the bridge in the centre, but from the sound-hole down thin the edges and the bottom of the lower bout to slightly less than 2mm. For normal size-range instruments I suggest that you do not go to less than 1.5mm. If cross grain is a problem, a fairly coarse abrasive sheet could be used instead of a plane but leave the last 0.2 mm of thickness for going down through grades of abrasive to give yourself a well-smoothed surface.

It is not possible to quote an exact thickness or gradation which will give optimum acoustic performance since every piece of wood is different in stiffness, gradation of annual ring lines and natural resonance. The dimensions I have suggested should be within normal tolerances for moderately good Spruce. Cedar could perhaps be a bit thicker by up to 25 per cent.

MAKING THE STRUTS

If this thickness of softwood had 35kg of string tension put upon it, it would not survive. It needs a reinforcement which both strengthens and spreads vibrations. This is called strutting. There are many patterns which have been used to arrange these struts and their various forms and ideas are considered later in this book. The slightly simplified version I recommend for a first guitar consists of five struts.

Each strut should start as a 230mm length of 6mm × 6mm light softwood cut so that the grain is straight along the piece and parallel to the sides at the endgrain. This may involve cutting and planing from a larger piece of timber to ensure straightness and grain direction. The exact method, of course, depends on the starting material but remember that straight grain can be produced by splitting larger pieces of timber approximately centrally. This can be used to give two good-sized pieces with a parallel-sided grain pattern which should make subsequent cutting straightforward. Sources were suggested in the chapter on Timber. Finished lengths are shown on the plan.

BRIDGE DIMENSIONS

The positions of these five struts depend on the position and dimensions of the bridge. The central area of the bridge consists of the saddle block and the string tie block. These are thicker and therefore more rigid than the thinner wings of the bridge. The main considerations of bridge design are covered in a later chapter but it is necessary to note here the more rigid central part and the less rigid wings. The bridge dimensions should be decided upon at this stage and the position and block outlines of the bridge drawn on the underside of the front as accurately as possible. The front edge of the saddle slot of a bridge (for 650mm scale length) should be 327.5mm from the top perimeter of the body. This is half the scale length plus 2–3mm for compensation (see Chapter 12). Draw the bridge in lightly but accurately. Crossbars support the front above and below the hole. Mark where these will come with their hole facing sides 10–15mm from the sound-hole edge.

CUTTING THE SOUND-HOLE

At this stage of marking out on the inside, the sound-hole can be cut. Using the inlay cutter trammelling around the centre hole with a sharp blade fitted flat side out (nearer the rosette), cut out the hole from both sides following the pattern of cutting a quarter circle at a time which was used in incising the inside of the rosette. Set the cutter to just over 2mm from the rosette interior edge.

POSITIONING AND GRADING THE STRUTS

With bridge and crossbars marked in light pencil lines the strut positions can be found. The third strut is central on the glue line. It runs from 5–6mm from the crossbar through the centre of the bridge and down to 15mm from the perimeter line.

Struts 2 and 4 pick up the edges of the bridge centre block. They should pass directly under the lower corners of the string tie block. They are pointed at the front top centre (i.e. The centre of the twelfth fret). Again they reach from 5–6mm from the cross bar to 15mm from the perimeter.

Struts 1 and 5 pick up the outer edge of the bridge wings and should pass under the points of the lower wing corners. Again, they point to top centre and they start and finish as the other struts.

The idea here is that triangles of graded rigidity are being created. Struts 2, 3 and 4 and the most substantial part of the bridge hold the peak of the dome as the most rigid area. Struts 1 and 5 and the whole bridge, including the more flexible wings, surround this with another fairly rigid larger triangle. The outer lower bout is less stiff and allows the central area some up and down movement which will be felt when the whole body is assembled. In this way, smaller stiffer areas are capable of responding to higher frequencies while not inhibiting progressively lower frequencies from being picked up by more flexible areas arranged

43

concentrically around them. This theory will apply while shaping the struts.

FRONT DOME

The front is not to be made flat but is to have a dome built into it. This does not mean that complex curves have to be cut in the timber members. All are made flat and the dome is placed in under stress and held by the glue drying. There are various benefits to this system. Principal among these is rigidity. The lower bout of the guitar is analogous to a loudspeaker cone. These are made of thin card (for lightness) and their necessary rigidity comes from the conical shape. This can readily be demonstrated on a flat sheet of paper. If you put a dot in the centre and cut a straight line to the edge you can pull the edges of the cut to overlap. Glue them in this way and you have remarkably increased rigidity with no increase of weight. This is essentially what

this system does with the very light wood of the guitar front.

Guitars which have been built with flat fronts often develop a depression between the bridge and the sound-hole and a dome below the bridge. This will not happen if this area, which might eventually distort downward is strengthened by distorting it upward. Less strutting is required to produce a stable top shape and this decreases weight which improves acoustic response. In addition the production of a domed front considerably eases the alignment geometry of other parts of the guitar. (This will be explained in the section on neck geometry in Chapter 10.)

PRESHAPING AND ATTACHING THE STRUTS

In order to attach the struts to the front in the domed shape it is first necessary to make a platen.

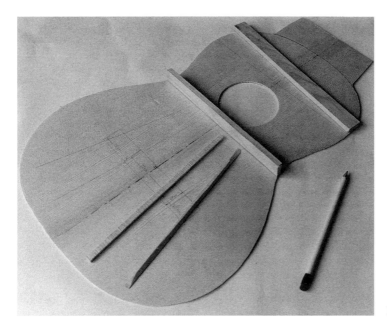

Planning the strutting.

To Make …

A FORMING PLATEN AND WEDGING GANTRY

This is a circle of approximately the diameter of the lower bout with a smooth depression in it of 7mm or so. I have turned an MDF platen to suit these dimensions (approximately 360mm) but my prototype was the seat of a kitchen stool. You may find you already have something ready made. If you do not have a suitable shape to hand and have no turning facilities, you can make this with layers of thick paper or card.

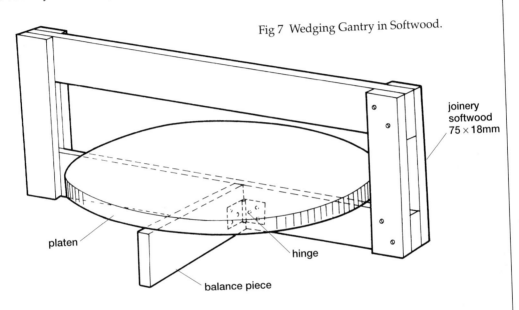

Fig 7 Wedging Gantry in Softwood.

joinery
softwood
75 × 18mm

platen

hinge

balance piece

A firm base is necessary, 380–400mm across. You will need a complete covering of 7mm thickness of card or paper. Card must be solid, not corrugated. Cut circles out of each layer of card to give a smooth inner curve. The first circle in the top layer should be 360mm. The lowest layer should have a hole in it revealing the base. I cannot be more specific without knowing what paper or card you are using. You are trying to create as smooth an internal curve as possible. The radius of this curve is 2.3m. Once cut, the layers must be glued and then their cut edges smoothed off.

You will need a framework over the platen against which wedges can be braced. The entire platen sits inside this framework and pairs of wooden wedges are used to force the front into the curvature while the glue on the wedged fan struts dries. This framework forms a gantry-like structure. It can be made from joinery softwood (as in the diagram) in 75mm × 18mm sections, or, as I have done, it can be cut out from a piece of thick plywood. There should be 35–50mm clear space between the platen top and the wedging gantry underside. Your wedges will probably need to be 15–25mm at the thick end and around 100mm long.

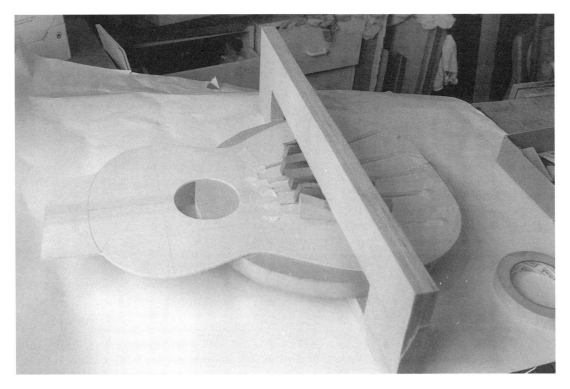

The platen and gantry in use gluing struts to the front.

Each fan strut can be cut to length and its position marked with the front lying flat. Light pencil numbers on the struts will help. The strut will be glued with the end-grain lines at right angles to the front timber. This gives maximum stiffness. It is usually suggested that the strut is glued in position first and that shaping the strut is done after the glue is dry. In practice, some of the shaping can usefully be done before gluing. The finished cross-section of a fan strut is a slightly domed triangle. Its deepest part, where it should be the full 6mm deep corresponds to the centre of the platen. The platen centre, which will give the summit of the dome, should be 15–25mm in front (i.e. hole side) of the centre of the bridge. So the struts can be preshaped by marking the deepest part (cross hatch the top) and cutting the sides away with chisel or plane to approach a triangular section. From the centre point of the dome the strut is to be tapered off both ways. Some smoothing and shaping will need to be done after the gluing as the wedges will leave some impression which will need to be smoothed out.

It is recommended that you practise the positioning of the struts and the wedging of them in place before you apply glue.

Place the front face down on the platen and ensure that a point 15–25mm in front of the centre of the bridge occupies the centre of the dome. The front can be taped in position around its edges. Place each strut in place and tape its ends in place

Apply sufficient glue to cause droplets of it to exude.

with strips of narrow masking tape. Apply pairs of wedges and, pressing the front into the centre of the dome by hand, squeeze the opposed wedges to hold the struts in place. Start with the central strut and, working fairly quickly, apply pairs of wedges to each of the struts. Check that they are in contact along their length.

When you are confident in this procedure you can begin gluing. Apply a single line of Titebond along the surface. Too much glue would leave an unworkmanlike mess and increase the tendency of the strut to slide out of place during wedging. Too little glue could give you sections of 'dry joint' between struts and top. This can have a disastrous effect on the tone and may cause buzzing. So apply sufficient glue to cause droplets of it to exude from every line between top and strut when wedged. Titebond shrinks markedly during drying so most of the excess glue exudate will become insignificant. If you do overdo the glue a bit, who will actually know?

I recommend that this arrangement is left overnight to dry. As the wedges are removed the bow in the assembly will spring back by about half its extent. This gives an overall dome from side to side of about 3.5mm.

FINISHING THE STRUTS

A sharp chisel (the carver's dog leg chisel is best) is used to shave the tops of the strutting to give a smooth finish where the wedges will have indented. Each strut is shaped to a domed triangle cross-section. Its highest point should be near to the centre of the doming of the front (15–25mm in front of the bridge). Toward the lower perimeter it is smoothed off into a long gradual curve tapering off to nil. Toward the hole it is tapered off to give a more rounded less gradual end. The image I have in mind is the top edge of an aerofoil section. A small metal or plastic ruler alongside the strut you are shaping may help prevent cutting into the front timber. Only the centre strut is left to its original 6mm height at the dome centre. The no 2 and 4 struts should be less. Struts 1 and 5 maximum height is smaller still.

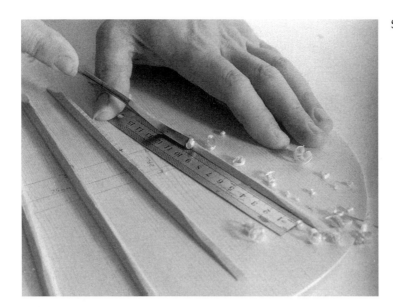

Shaping the struts …

… and sanding them off.

Final smoothing of the struts with abrasive sheet is advisable and here again strips of protective material e.g. modeller's ply alongside the struts will help. Try to smooth off to remove all chisel mark edges and obtain flowing continuous curves.

POSITIONING THE CROSSBARS

Next, the crossbars should be glued in place. These will be of the same material as the strutting and approximately 10mm wide by 15–18mm deep. The grain must run in the same direction as specified for the fan struts. A majority of the shaping into a dome topped or domed triangle cross section can be done before gluing. Glue each bar to the pencil marks already made, held in place with masking tape under a weight. Do not forget the precautions necessary in placing the front face down on a workboard. Ensure that glue droplets can be seen along the whole length. A section of 'dry joint' here would be serious.

REINFORCING THE ROSETTE HOLE

Finally, it is necessary to reinforce the edges of the hole where the timber has nearly been cut through in inlaying the rosette. A paper template can be made and adjusted to give a constant distance from the inside of the hole of 3–4mm. This template is then used to cut two pieces from the scrap remains from the front blank. Note that it is not necessary to glue these on to the two crossbars and it will be seen

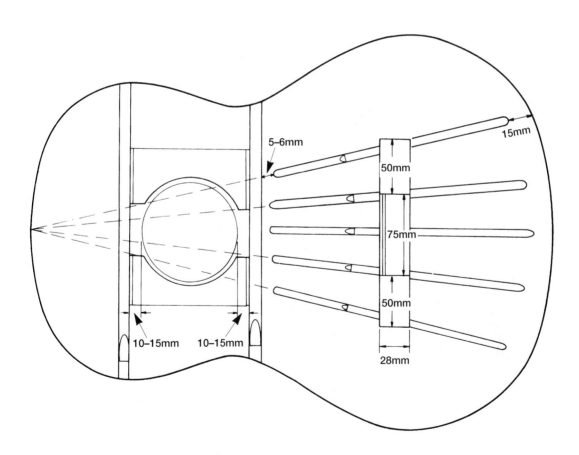

Fig 8 Front layout.

that I have chamfered them away at this point so that they do not touch. These pieces can be thinned to 3mm or so and should be rounded on all edges before gluing. Ensure that a large flat weight presses them down over their entire surface while glue dries. A non-adhered part anywhere on the front could be a problem later.

Final removal of the scrap handling piece on the upper bout to the perimeter line completes the front assembly.

To Make ...

A BRIDGE CAUL

Before putting this aside it is a good time to make the bridge caul. This is a piece of wood used to brace the bridge when gluing. It needs, therefore, to be a good fit to the bridge area underside. Take a piece of softwood just slightly larger than the bridge and at least 18mm thick. Carefully mark the position of the struts and cut out with a tenon saw so that the caul drops over the struts without touching them in the marked bridge position. Leave a little more space than necessary for the outer struts. The caul will need to be shaped to the front curvature later on.

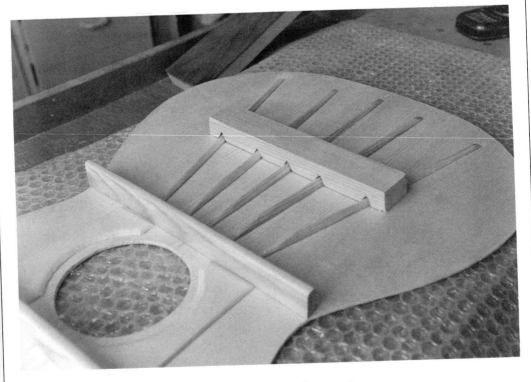

The bridge caul in place – note also the sound-hole reinforcements.

6 The Back

JOINTING AND THICKNESSING

Apart from being made of hardwood the back blank resembles the front blank and many of the processes used on it are therefore the same.

It is worth having an exploratory plane at each piece before jointing. If there is some difficulty in planing them both in the same direction then some thinning should be done before jointing. If not, it is as easy to plane the whole back as one piece. Jointing the back on its centre line differs in no material way from the treatment of the front.

If the timber is an oily or resinous exotic, it is worth doing some glue testing on corner scraps. Some timbers glue better if thoroughly wiped with turpentine and allowed to dry on gluing surfaces first.

When the piece is jointed it should be planed smooth on its outer surface. This will be chosen for the best grain match and should be done before cutting the piece out to the plan outline. Again, leave a handling piece along the top of the upper bout of some 40mm or more if the best grain match positioning allows. This is best done by laying the mould on the back and moving it back and forth to get the best effect.

Once cut out, plane and scrape the outer surface to a good finish before turning over and thicknessing. The thickness of the back will depend on its density. Dense timbers require to be taken down to about 2–2.5mm thickness to give sufficient lightness to the finished instrument. However, taking less

dense timbers down to these dimensions can reduce the projection of the sound of the guitar and thus its apparent sound volume.

If less dense timbers need to be thicker perhaps it is the overall weight of the back which has some ideal value? I cannot answer this with any certainty but I have weighed backs when I have considered them about right and, for this size of guitar I find I am often near to 250g. If you have no means of this kind of weighing then I can offer generalizations. Dense timbers such as rosewoods I find come out satisfactorily at about 2.25mm. Walnut seems happy at about 3mm while Sycamore and Mahogany I tend to give 3.3mm. It is easy when planing on a flat surface with the thickness only visible on the edge to leave the middle a little thicker. I believe that this does no harm and so I tend to allow a little less than I have specified at the very edge and check that the middle, especially right behind the hole, is just a bit more.

SUPPORT BARS

The back of a guitar is not flat but has a domed shape in both width and length. The dome across the width is held in place by the curve cut into the edge of the three struts across it. The dome in length does not take effect until the final assembly.

The back struts can be made of hard or softwood. They need to be reasonably light and to be cut in a direction which gives maximum rigidity. The same softwood recommended for front crossbars and strutting can be used. Mahogany and hardwood Cedar can also be used and it may be that you will have sufficient scrap for this from the sides of your neck blank.

Crossbars need to be 10mm wide and 15–18mm deep, the largest, the lower bout bar being the deepest. The lower bout bar is positioned at the widest point of the lower bout. The upper bout bar is also positioned at the widest point of its bout. The middle bar is usually approximately half way between the other two. Draw positions for all three bars on your guitar back.

It is desirable to get a good even curve on the bars and to make a caul which will hold them accurately while glue dries. To do this, mark a curve of radius 3 metres. Fix one end of a metal tape and place a loop of masking tape over it at 3m. Make a pencil point hole in this and you will be able to mark the curve. If you take the wedging gantry you made with the platen

for doming the front and mark this curve on its bottom inner edge, it can be shaved away with a spokeshave to the drawn line. This curve can then be transferred accurately to the crossbars so that they can be planed to correct shape. The bars can be glued in place one at a time across the back using wedges such as you used to fix the fan struts. The resulting curve should be about 5mm across the lower bout. Some makers increase the curve on the middle back strut to give a more peaked curve to the back as a whole. A curvature of about 2m radius comes out about right.

JOINT REINFORCEMENT

It is customary to strengthen the centre joint further on the inside of the instrument. This is done with what is called 'crossbanding'. This is meant to signify that the grain in these strips of wood runs

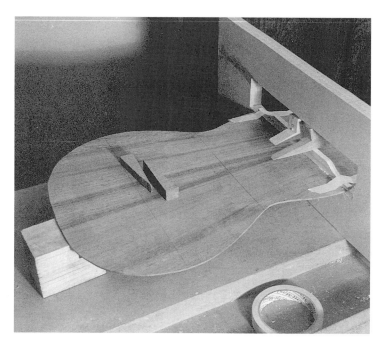

Fitting the back struts with a curved-bottomed wedging gantry.

Stages in shaping crossbanding.

at right angles to the grain in the timber of the back. This does effectively reduce the chance of a split in the centre joint running down the back and separating the two halves. You don't need to look in many guitars before you realize that some makers add a centre strip in which the grain runs lengthways. There is little point in this as it would split with the joint.

Crossbanding is not all that difficult (and, in any case, there is an easier method for the lazy!). Take the scrap timber from around the back and cut the longest strips you can across the grain about 15mm wide. For ease of handling these should be lightly glue-tacked on tiny dots of Titebond to the edge of a strip of narrower wood such as your 12 × 25mm softwood. This can then be held in

the vice while you plane or chisel away the edges to give a lens-shaped cross-section about 2mm thick. Smooth this off nicely with abrasive sheet. This can then be lifted with a palette knife and cut into lengths to fit between crossbars one and two and two and three. Leave the piece below the third crossbar and the bottom block to be fitted later. Ensure that these are fitted accurately central and taped and weighted until the glue is dry. These crossbandings could be done in the same timber as the crossbars or in some contrasting timber to good effect.

For the lazy (yes, I put my hand up) they can be done very well in 15mm strips of 1.5mm modeller's ply cut across the grain. See the later chapter on linings – you may have a lot of this as scrap.

FINISHING

Decide before you trim the back to its finished outline whether you are going to cap the heel in a separate piece of timber or continue the back timber over it. If the latter you must leave enough to cover the heel piece. Final trimming occurs later.

The crossbars need to be rounded over and sanded and scalloped at the end. The last 25–30mm is chiselled out to a curve leaving a thickness of 6mm at the perimeter.

Scalloping crossbar ends.

(*Below*) The back finished one side and crossbanded.

7 The Sides

The preparation and processing of the sides of the instrument are probably the most demanding tasks in terms of accuracy in the whole procedure.

As with the other paired pieces of timber, it is necessary to find the two matching faces and deal with these first. It is also essential to know the finished size you need and this cannot be done simply by overlaying the mould on them.

LENGTH AND DEPTH

To find the finished length you need to prepare, run a tape-measure around the inside of one half of the mould. Hold it against the inside wall, possibly with masking tape as you go. Add 60mm at each end of this length to allow for cramping to the workboard and later for trimming. Ensure that your blank is long enough to accommodate this. Decisions about the width of each piece need to be taken. Much the best procedure is to make up a side template of stiff card or modeller's ply.

The length is the side length plus 120mm. The width is rather arbitrary. No two makers have the same depth measurements. The normal practice is for the bottom to be approximately 10mm deeper than the heel. I suggest an instrument 90mm deep at the heel and 100mm deep at the bottom. It must be realized that these are the side measurements plus the top and bottom thickness. If we subtract 3mm for the back thickness and 2mm for the top thickness then we require to finish the sides 5mm less than the instrument's finished dimensions. That is 85mm at the heel and 95mm at the bottom.

One edge of the template should be a straight edge. This is the front edge. The edge which will join to the back requires a slight curvature from 95mm down to 85mm but leaving 250mm parallel at the 95mm end. This is given in the diagram below.

PLANING AND TRIMMING

To begin planing down the sides, the workboard should be cramped down to the

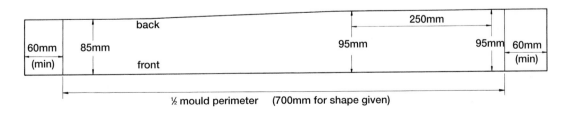

Fig 9 Side Template.

Planing down a side.

(*Left*) Note the use of the work-board overhang.

work-bench with the 100mm overhang on the working side. This overhang allows the side to be G-cramped down at the centre of one end. It is advisable to plane and scrape down the side which will form the outside of the instrument to a good finish on both pieces before cutting it down to the template shape. Always cramp the side down at the near end and plane away from this. The same applies to scraping. If cross grain makes this impossible with the plane then the scraper should be used and a finish will need to be obtained with abrasive sheets.

When the outer faces have a satisfactory finish, attach them together with strips of masking tape finished faces out. Draw around the template with a 2B pencil and cut out to shape. This is where the motorized fretsaw or the band saw come into their own. If you do not have either of these, a coping saw will do the back edge working between battens, with a short plane to finish. Finish the front edge with a long plane.

You now have your sides with one side finished, both edges trimmed and 60mm scrap still present at each end.

Cramp one of them down, as before, with the inner surface uppermost. This is the surface that has not been worked on yet. This surface must be planed and or scraped until it is the same thickness, to within very close limits over its whole surface. But what thickness? Here again there are no absolute answers. This depends on the density of the wood as well as its natural ability to bend on the heating iron (*see* below). Denser timbers tend to be taken down thinner for reasons of finished weight. I usually take Indian Rosewood down to 1.5mm. Cypress for flamenco guitars should be the same. Lighter timbers such as Mahogany and Walnut can be left thicker and should be fine at 2mm. Because of the risk of scorch marks on the hot iron I suggest that blonde timbers such as the Maples should be just a bit thinner at around 1.75mm. This may cause some Maple types to ripple slightly along the length and this means applying internal 'rib' pieces in the finished instrument. Fortunately you have some scrap (the pieces you have cut from the sides) on which to try the bending process. Use these to practise the heat bending and you will gain some experience and may be able to decide for yourself if the thickness needs to be modified.

In planing the sides you will need extreme care and patience to obtain the thickness you need without taking any

Final thicknessing with a scraper.

part down too thin. I recommend that you aim at the finished thickness plus 0.2mm and take this last bit off with a scraper blade. Be aware that you are likely when planing to leave the middle of the piece too thick, but that when scraping the middle is likely to come down more quickly than the sides. Very frequent checking with the thickness gauge is essential. Mark thicker or thinner areas with pencil to guide your work. When scraping, beware of the edges on your knuckles holding the blade as scraped edges can be razor sharp. Your first experience of taking sides down to correct thickness may take a couple of hours or more (each!) but it is still a small fraction of the overall time so don't get impatient.

HEAT BENDING

To bend the sides it is necessary to set up a hot tube. Pictures from the workshops of the old-time luthiers of Spain show them leaning against sides pressed to the hood of the heating brazier. I always wondered what they did in the summer? In this more electrical age we can buy heated tubes set up for the purpose and thermostatically controlled. Unfortunately, these are not cheap and so for a first try at least, something a little more makeshift is likely to be tried. My own solution seems to work well and costs little.

Once set up, I recommend a bit of practice with pieces of the scrap from the sides and with modeller's ply. The tube may heat up too much. If it does, cool it down with a couple of squirts of water mist from a small garden sprayer.

Having had some practice, I suggest that you now give some thought to the procedure you are going to adopt on these two pieces of timber as they probably

To Make ...

A HEAT-BENDING TUBE

As may be seen from the photograph, I have set a hot-air paint stripper in to the end of a 300–400mm length of 50–60mm steel tubing held in wooden blocks in a vice. Set up as shown, it takes a couple of minutes to heat up and is hot enough when a drop of water bounces off with a slight 'ping'.

The heat-bending tube set up.

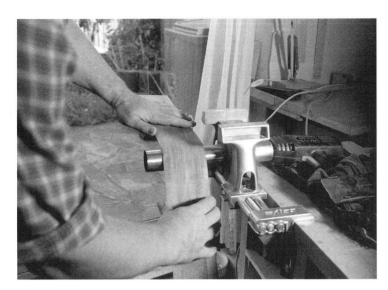

Bending the sides starts at the waist.

represent several hour's work by now. Make sure that the ends clearly show the 60mm waste. Find the distance from this of the centre point of the waist curvature and pencil mark this on the inner side.

I tend to bend dark timbers dry and to soak blonde timbers to avoid scorch marks. Soaking timbers involves submerging them in a bath of cold water for 20 minutes or so. Do not soak for more extended periods or grain can become very difficult and fray on the outside of curves. Rosewoods may start to exude boiling resin on heated surfaces so soaking or just spraying these may be advisable. Decide for yourself using pieces of the scrap. If you do soak the timber for bending you will need to allow time for the water to evaporate before gluing them. This can be checked if you have accurate weighing facilities; otherwise, it should be left for a week to ten days to ensure that shrinking has ceased.

Bending over the heating iron requires some practice and skill acquisition so I have stressed practice on scrap and/or ply. Before starting you need to be clearly aware of which is the inner and outer surfaces, the front and back and whether you have the upper or lower side in your hand. Have the mould, front side down on the bench in front of you. It should have its neck complete and be without backboard.

Apply the waist to the iron first. Rocking or sliding motions of the side on the heated tube are the method of controlling the degree and sharpness of bend. Place the side on without movement and it will quickly bend to a very sharp curve. Rock it constantly and the curve will be more gradual. Try to match the curve to the waist of the mould by constant comparison. On either side of the waist curvature there will be a short straight section. Turn the side over and follow the lower bout curvature. Keep everything moving; the side must be a smooth curve and not resemble the old threepenny bit. It is too easy to get a series of kinks rather than a curve. It is also necessary to keep the axis of the side at right angles to the bending iron or you can produce a corkscrew. Some straightening will take place on cooling so

Use the mould as a template.

you may need to cool everything off for an hour and see what happens. This will not make it any more difficult to reheat and correct curvature again later but wetted timbers will need spraying if this is done.

FINISHING

When you are satisfied that you have two sides as identical as you can make them, you need to brace them into the mould

with thin garden canes and postage-stamp-sized pieces of modeller's ply. Start at the waist and ensure that both sides are a reasonable fit. Cut a piece of thin garden cane which will just reach across this waist gap and spring it into place, protecting each end with a square of the thin ply. Repeat this in the upper bout and the lower bout. Put another cane length in longways. It will be holding two overlapping waste ends at this stage. Check whether any parts of the upper or lower bouts can be pressed in to the mould shape by hand. Turn the mould on its side and check visually how good a fit you have between the front edges of the sides and the mould outline.

If no further heat bending is needed to satisfy you then you can cut through to trim the sides to length along the centre line of the mould top and bottom and remove the scrap pieces. The centre line at the top bout will be trimmed again later. The bottom joint is as it will be glued but subsequently gets a cover of inlay work.

Congratulations! I think you've just finished the hardest bit. The sides can now be left in the mould until they are needed for assembly.

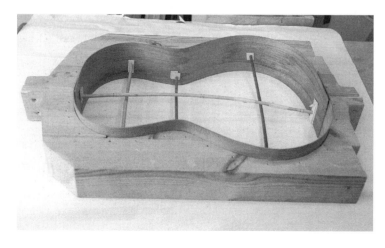

The sides completed.

8 The Head and Neck

Considerable variation is found in construction and procedure as well as in aesthetics of design. Traditionally the head and neck are scarfed together at the head – neck joint and at the heel which is built up from a series of layers. The length of the neck itself is a single piece. However, some people choose to build the heel of a single block and some make the neck and heel of a single continuous piece. This latter would seem to involve a lot of waste. Strengthening to the neck can be provided by the insertion of a 10mm square steel tube centrally under the fingerboard. This has much to commend it if you have the necessary router and bit to do it.

The piece from which you start needs to be about 75mm × 25mm and 1metre long. Ideally, the grain should be at right angles to the 75mm face and straight along the length of the piece.

SCARF JOINTING

The first operation is to scarf the head piece on to the back of the neck. To avoid later problems a good deal of design planning has to be done, so I recommend that you start at the drawing-board.

The first decision is about the head angle. A fairly low angle was traditional – as little as 6 degrees – but this has increased in modern guitars and I am going to recommend 12 degrees as about the most acceptable today. Draw it – disagree if you like, but decide now.

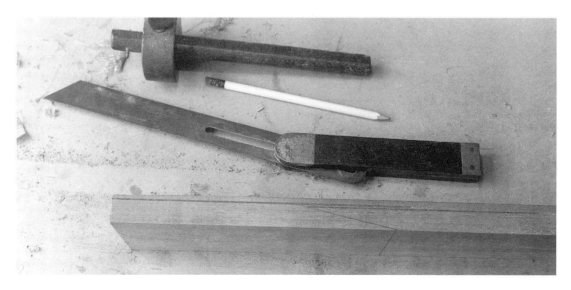

Planning a correctly placed scarf joint.

Although a supplied neck blank is about 25mm thick, if we scarf it at this thickness the joint will show and it is better to conceal it. The top end of the neck is going to be about 15mm deep when finished. The head will be given a decorative front (I am going to recommend a 3mm thickness piece out of the back timber) and needs to end up 20–22mm thick. So the head piece needs 17–19mm thickness and is going to be cut from the end of the neck piece. Once scarfed on (*see* diagram below) the joint is going to be lost in the curvature between the head and the neck. All of this should be drawn out on paper to determine thicknesses and confirm that they will give the desired alignment.

According to this diagram, it is necessary to trim down the end from which the head will be cut to about 18mm thickness over a length of more than 200mm. After cutting off the head piece at the desired angle as shown, the neck end needs to be

planed down further to about 16mm before planing the cut surface of the head piece and scarfing it on as explained below. Check that this alignment works on paper, most especially if you wish to change any parameter, e.g the head veneer thickness or the scarf angle.

So cut and/or plane the necessary thickness down to the point of the scarf cut. Set up a sliding bevel if you have one, mark the line of cut on all four surfaces and cut it off, being particularly careful with the thinner parts of the wedge shape. Plane the cut surface of the headpiece to a perfect flat (or cheat if you have a large disc sander!). Go on planing the back of the neck to 16mm and ensure a good flat surface for the scarf to the head.

Cramping angled scarf joints with glue in is asking for trouble as the glue-lubricated joint will slide; a little more forward planning is needed so that we can hold the joint with screws. Plan where the string slots in

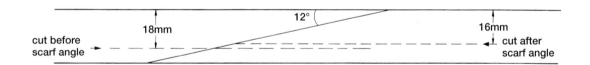

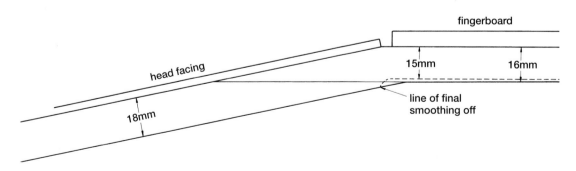

Fig 10 Planning the head–neck scarf.

(*Above*) Planning the stringslots shows the waste which can be used to screw the joint together.

Scarf joint screwed and cramped.

the head are going to come. Remember that the lower front part of the head still has to be planed. When you can rough out with a pencil where the slots come you can drill through with a 2.5mm drill, give a 4.5mm clearance hole in the front of the neck section and screw the pieces together with two 25mm no. 8 screws. Position a neck screwcramp above and below the screws and check for fit all round. Dismantle and reassemble with a sparing layer of Titebond.

When this is hard, remove the cramps and plane the head front to a smooth flat surface ensuring that the angle between the head and neck front surfaces runs at right angles across the neck front.

This line will represent the back edge of the nut. I recommend a nut thickness of 5mm. Mark the nut thickness across and you have the line that represents the start of the fingerboard. From this, mark half the string length (recommended 325mm) down the neck and you have the position of the neck – body joint. A further 90mm on down the neck is the approximate position of the first crossbar in the front. I recommend that you cut across at this point. (I should point out that carrying the neck down inside the body as far as this is a departure from the purely traditional, which would be some 50mm less.)

STEEL TUBE REINFORCEMENT

At this point the square steel tube can be inserted if desired. It may be felt that this will be a noticeable weight addition to the instrument. But 300mm of such tube weighs, I discover, about 100g. It replaces just over 33 cubic centimetres of Mahogany at a specific gravity of about 0.55, a weight of about 18g. A net increase of 82g or so in the overall weight is the result.

A 10mm router bit is required. The channel should be started from 50mm below the start of the string length. It should be routed in several passes to about 10.2mm depth ensuring that it is central. Clean all four sides of the steel tube with a file before bedding it in with a layer of epoxy-resin on the bottom and sides of the channel.

BUILDING THE HEEL BLOCK

At this stage, the remains of the neck piece can be cut and jointed up to form the heel. This is another stage where I recommend you consult your drawing board. You have the neck piece with the neck – body joint marked. I shall suggest that the heel piece continues on down to the first crossbar across the back. This is another slight

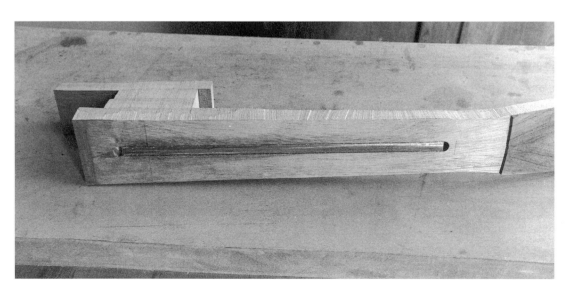

10mm square steel tube routed in.

(*Right*) Plan the heel before cutting and gluing.

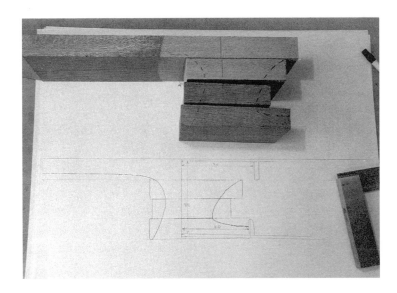

Fig 11 Planning the heel block and heel design.

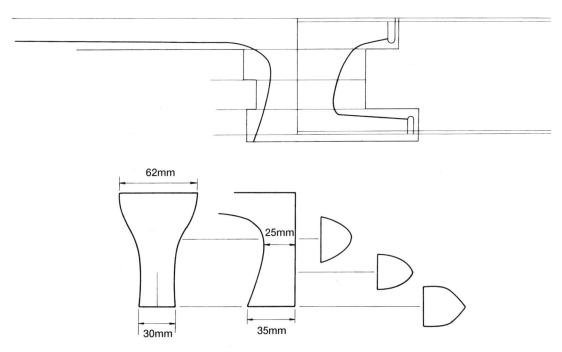

62mm

25mm

30mm

35mm

departure from the tradition although I am not the first to do it. Draw in longitudinal section the neck – body joint area as you wish it to be, draw in the crossbars which exist on your back and your front, and then decide how to cut your remaining neck timber best to suit.

Once cut, each piece will need to be planed to join it to the piece above and below, although, once again, if you have a

65

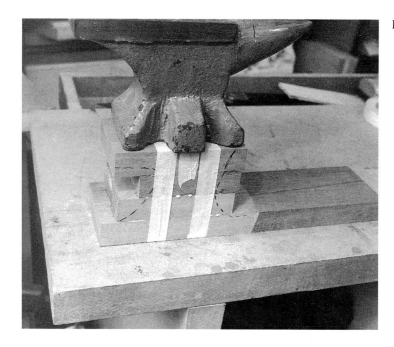

Heel block gluing.

large disc sander this is easier. Hold the pieces firmly in place with masking tape to avoid slipping, and place them under a fairly heavy weight.

HEAD DESIGN AND DECORATION

In order to design and cut out the head and neck shape you will need a centre line drawn down the front of the head and neck. Ensure that it remains a straight line over the angle between head and neck.

Machine Heads

In order to design the head it is necessary to know the dimensions of all parts of the machine heads. There is a very wide choice of machine heads available today and a great range of price. The most expensive can be a hundred times the price of the cheapest! However the same probably applies to guitars.

The cheaper construction method for machine heads consists of bending the backplate forward to provide the retainers and bearing surfaces of the worm gear. This can only provide a small bearing surface and is prone to wear. The more expensive and, indeed, most expensive types have the bearing capstans rivetted on to the backplates. It is worth looking closely at this type to see if they have rivet extending behind the backplate. If they do, this will necessitate depressions being cut in the head before the backplate will lie flush with the woodwork. At least one manufacturer of reasonably priced machine heads creates a one piece bearing surface and backplate assembly, presumably by folding and welding, which seems structurally ideal and reduces play to an absolute minimum.

The amount of play in a machine head needs to be assessed with the assembly off the instrument. The plastic roller should wiggle by a very small amount, if at all. The roller should not rotate perceptibly without the tuning key being turned. The tuning key, usually of some sort of plastic, should not move on its shaft at all. Some tuning keys have screws holding them on. There is nothing wrong with this as long as the player remembers the occasional check on tightness. The tuning key should turn smoothly with the same resistance for a full rotation of the roller (14 or 16 turns depending on gearing). The worst fault, not easy to discern, is the roller which is excentric on its axis, which would warrant returning the machine head for replacement.

In designing the head it is necessary to study the dimensions of the machine heads. One simple example: the length of the screws supplied will govern the thickness of the side section of the head. If, as in some cases, the screws are longer than you want, you would need to discard them and try a modeller's supplier for smaller screws to fit.

The size and spacing of the rollers is the most critical point and here it seems a shame that there is no absolute standard of diameter and spacing. There is, however, a most common size and I would strongly recommend using it to ensure later interchangeability. A majority of manufacturers make 10mm rollers which are set at 35mm centres. This size is found at a variety of price ranges and seems to have no drawbacks to make it worth departing from. The problems of replacing old machine heads whose size cannot be duplicated, especially on roller centres spacing, are considerable.

Before going further with the head design, the front of the head is to be faced off with a decorative layer. Again, the variation is enormous but I am going to suggest that you probably have sufficient scrap back material to face the head and that this

Machine heads. Top to bottom: folded, rivetted and one-piece.

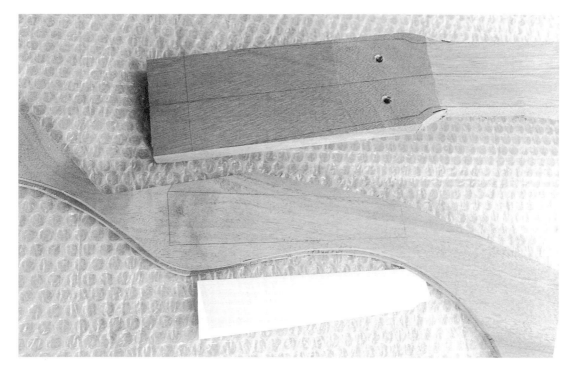

Marking out head veneers from back scrap.

will tie the overall colour design scheme together most effectively.

Make a folded paper plan of the finished head. Take the two scrap sections from around the back and place them together so that their grain matches. Lay your folded head plan on them and find a place where a piece can be cut from both layers that will give you an interesting book match at the centre line of the head. Plane these pieces smooth where they will glue to the head and cut them out. Plane them along the centre joint to make a good fit and glue them together to the front of the head. They can be taped together and taped to the head to hold them in place, and cramped with your four neck screwcramps.

Later, with the glue dry, you can plane them off to 3mm or so and draw or tape

your head design on and carefully cut the outline of the sides out. At this stage, cut out the neck outline as well. The width should be 50–52mm at the nut and 62mm at the neck – body junction. Draw this in pencil and cut without encroaching on the line; final trimming comes much later.

The front of the head section is some 200mm long by 75mm wide and should have a centre line down it. At the head – neck angle the neck should be 50–52mm wide allowing a fingerboard top of 2–3mm more than this, i.e. 52–55mm. Mark this in pencil either side of the centreline. The first string roller should be about 40mm from the head–neck angle. Place your machine head on at about this position. Mark the position of the front of the sideplate and mark a width of about 65mm at this level.

(*Right*) Gluing head veneers. Note a decorative light veneer interleaf is included.

(*Below*) Planning the head with respect to the machine heads.

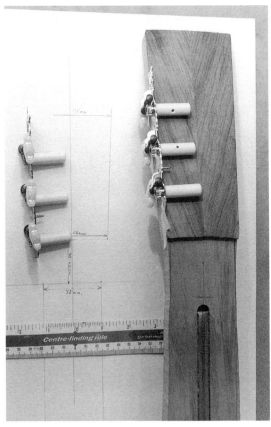

At a few millimetres above the top end of the sideplate mark the full width of 75mm across the head. This should give you a line for the sides of the head. Line these in in pencil. Now you can draw out your head design on paper. Consider your machine head screws and decide on your side bar width. This may need to be a chunky 10mm if the screws are long or a delicate 7mm if you can get screws which will fit, or anything in between.

Now consider how far past this the hole in the roller comes. It is really nice if the hole in the roller is in the middle of the string slot and not off to one side. Measure your machine head and see what sort of string slot this suggests. Draw this on your paper plan. I suggest that the string slot should extend at least 15mm past the rollers at each end. Some people make this gap very small and third and fourth strings become more fiddly to fit.

The top of the string slot is always semi-circular and the bottom end usually is, too. Draw these in on your plan.

69

When it comes to the shape of the top of the head there are more variations than could be recorded in a book this size, but when designing it remember that you've got to cut it. It is not necessary to use the whole of the 200mm length. A design suggestion is given in Figure 12.

The head drilling and cutting and the cutting of the neck – body joint are two separate operations which can be done in either order.

DRILLING AND CUTTING THE HEAD

It is absolutely essential that the holes for the tuning rollers are accurately spaced, in a straight line and correctly distanced from the front of the head. It is difficult to know how to specify a method when there are so many ways of drilling holes. The size of the drill needs to give a hole with some clearance around the rollers. Check the rollers on your machine heads. A drill of 10.5mm is needed for 10mm rollers.

I suggest that you take a piece of hardwood scrap approximately 30mm × 30mm cross-section and do your best to drill holes at accurate 35mm centres. If you succeed, your machine heads will slip into the holes with an excellent fit and no slack, from both sides. When you can drill a block of wood sufficiently accurately to fulfil this specification you can use the block as a drilling guide. Plane one edge to give a regular distance of 12mm from the hole centres and glue it by this surface to a piece of substantial ply about 10cm square. This can be cramped to the front of the head, spaced off with veneer or ply shims as required and used to guide the drilling of

A variety of head designs.

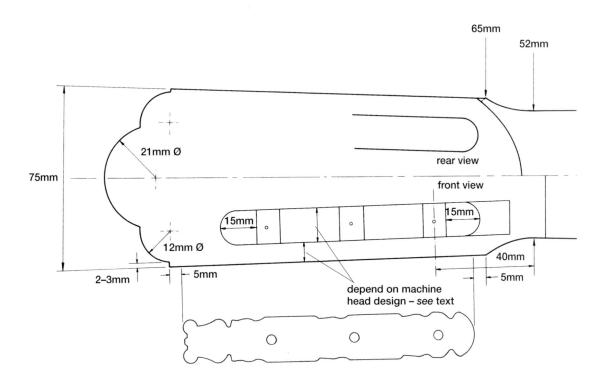

65mm

52mm

21mm Ø

rear view

front view

75mm

15mm

15mm

12mm Ø

40mm

2–3mm

5mm

5mm

depend on machine
head design – *see* text

Fig 12 Suggested head design,
front and rear.

Holes drilled to a good fit in
hardwood scrap.

Scrap piece of wood used as a drill guide. Note the paper shims for spacing.

accurate holes. Work out the depth of hole needed to drop the roller in without binding on the end and mark this with masking tape on your drill bit. You may find that the first and sixth holes join up as one. If necessary, roller ends can be filed but you may prefer to take the opportunity to redesign the head if you foresee this happening.

The profile of the top of the head can be cut with a fret or coping saw and filed and sanded to shape. Check with your paper plan that this is accurately symmetrical.

Place the back of the head against a firm flat surface of scrap timber to drill down vertically through the string slot as drawn on the front. You may wish to drill out the ends of the slots accurately with the correct sized drill or prefer to drill out undersize and saw or file back to the line. Cut the rest of the slot out with a fret or coping saw.

The nut end of the string slots is chamfered out to about half the depth or a little more. This can be done with a square ramp or with a good carver's gouge the drilled hole can be continued into a semi-circular ramp. Other shapes are also possible. Check that when the nut is in place, the strings would pass to their rollers without making contact with the woodwork.

CUTTING THE BODY JOINT AND HEEL

Cramp the neck face down and with two set squares and a ruler establish a centre

(*Above*) Cutting the string slots after drilling. Recognize the fretting table?

Cutting ramps straight across.

line along the heel. From this centre line mark a width of 40mm along the heel area. The top surface of the neck should be cut out such that at the neck – body junction it is 62mm wide. Mark this width parallel along the remainder of this end of the neck. With a panel saw, or bandsaw if you have one, cut between these lines top and bottom. Mark the position of the neck – body junction all the way round.

There are, in fact, several ways of making this joint. Traditionally the joint was made up of slots cut to the width of the side thickness. The sides are simply pushed in after glue application. Cutting slots of exactly the same thickness can be tricky, as can sliding the sides in inside the mould. You can do this but I have another suggestion.

There is another time honoured method used by at least one of the world's great luthiers. The joint is simply a tapered dovetail tenon matching into a dovetail mortise in a separate block of wood built into the body. This method is used on most steel-string guitars as a mass-production technique but by hand it complicates neck alignment.

My own method involves a little more cutting and the making of a wedging block but is quite straightforward. Find the angle the perimeter of the body makes with the neck sides. Mark this angle in to near the centre. It is likely to be around 3–6 degrees. With a tenon saw, cut along the neck – body line and ensure that the cut is following the marked angle top and bottom (this would, in any case be the start of the first method as well). Cut to within 5–6mm of the heel centre line and about 10–12mm of the neck centre line. From the end of this cut, plot a line, top and bottom, that goes into the body side at 45 degrees and plot it up the side. Now you are ready to cut a loose wedge out from both sides which is not exacting in its measurements and yet will glue back in eventually to a perfect tight fit. Mark the faces of the wedges and their adjacent surfaces on the body side to avoid confusion later. Set these aside in a safe place.

This method also has the advantage of cutting timber back away from the heel and making the heelpiece much more accessible to your shaping tools.,

At this stage it is back to the drawing of this area that you did earlier in order to mark where you must cut the heel and the piece interior to the body from the side. Mark these and cut them out with a coping saw. Leave a little on the bottom end of the

Centre lining the heel.

My suggested wedge joint variation on the traditional.

(*Below*) Cutting the heel block profile.

heel and its block in the body to be cut to size later.

Cutting the elegant shape of the heel, blending it in to the shape of the neck and keeping everything symmetrical is another one of those rather tricky bits! There is only one way to proceed at this the first time round – slowly.

I have done this with a round Surform and rasps. I have done some of it with ordinary chisels and I have often had recourse to coarse abrasive sheet. I have even tried a powerfile. I have settled on a rather large carver's skew chisel as the best for me. With all of them it is a slow and painstaking job.

Plan the shape of the heel end first. Again there are a variety of styles and I merely suggest one. Remember that a little bit gets planed off this later. Cut back to the edges of this in stages and establish a slight concave curve from here down not

Heel shaping with a carver's skew chisel.

quite to meet the side of the front of the neck. I suggest cramping it neck-face down to the bench. If you have a profile gauge it helps with this; otherwise, put a piece of white paper into both wedge slots and view from the end at frequent intervals. Never try to take off more than a thin shaving at a time or you may break bits of short grain off the heel side.

I always combine this operation with the shaping of the neck, although some will tell you that this has to be left till later. I don't feel that this runs into any problems, as we shall see.

SHAPING THE NECK

One of the most important things with the neck is to get a smooth continuous slight taper from about 15mm behind the nut to about 18 or 19mm behind the ninth fret where the swell into the heel occurs. There is a straightforward way of establishing this first. The distance of this smooth taper is about 270mm. I have taken two strips of hardwood and planed this taper on to them over this distance and then fixed them down to an MDF backboard parallel at about 220mm distance. Between these are two narrower strips so that the neck can be wedged face down and planed to this taper with the long plane. Once sized, the plane can remove no more timber.

Shaping the neck is best done with a spokeshave. A profile gauge helps here, too, but much of it has to be done by feel. Do not remove anything from the centre line of the planed section until you are right down to final smoothing off. Do not

Thicknessing the neck in a home-made jig.

Shaping the neck with spokeshaves.

remove timber from the very side of the neck face as this has to be left until after the fingerboard is in place.

FINISHING

Finally, the back of the head needs shaping and blending in to the back of the neck. I use the skew chisel again here to ensure that a pleasing shape is established which drops the end of the scarf joint between head and neck into the curve at the bottom edge of the back of the head.

The heelpiece needs to be sanded to a good finish now as this is more difficult later. The cut surfaces of the neck parts interior to the body also need to be sanded as this part will be visible through the hole. Check that the interior of the heel is correct for depth. Always check back with your drawing.

Check the thickness of the front where it joins the neck. This thickness needs to be removed from the front of the neck timber where it continues inside the body so that the neck and front fit together without a step of level. If you have fitted the square steel tube you will need to cut out a piece from the front as well. Mark the front thickness on a marking gauge all round the neck block and pare off with a chisel. The two need to be perfectly level across the front where the fingerboard will fit.

Showing cutaways to fit front and neck flush. Note also the heel side shape.

9 Linings

I mentioned in the first chapter that the guitar is made without the interlocking joints that characterize furniture construction. Guitar sides may be as little as 1.5mm thick and are held to the front and back by glue alone. Linings increase the gluing area in these internal corners of the box. They should be light and they have to be capable of being applied to the curvature of the side but they make no particular contribution, in my opinion, to the acoustics so just what they are made of is of little significance.

I distinguish four ways of creating linings. Three of these are applied to the sides before joining the sides to the front.

KERFED LININGS

The idea of these linings is to create a straight-grained strip of wood, usually a

The very simple kerfing mitre box.

right-angled triangle in cross-section, and to cut through this with a saw to leave about half a millimetre of thickness of wood on the longest right-angle adjacent side. This leaves the whole strip flexible in one plane. Almost any light timber can be used. The small section joinery softwood recommended elsewhere is excellent. It should be cut and planed to a triangle 6–8mm × 10–12mm. With a band-saw, two of these can be had from the section normally supplied of about 10 × 22mm. Cutting kerfed linings is a repetitive job and one where I have always found background music essential!

You have to decide how close the cuts have to come to conform to the curves you require. Try an experimental piece with the kerfing jig on the inside of your mould where the corners of the upper bout are usually the tightest internal curve. This lining is glued to your side, in the mould, with clothes pegs holding it in place after the sides and neck are joined. Further details are in the following chapter. Meanwhile support the strip with a length of masking tape along the kerfed face for ease of handling.

HEAT BENDING

This lining is essentially a narrow piece of side. It may be part of the scrap from the side itself but is often a contrasting piece of timber. It can be a little thicker than the side to increase its gluing area. It is bent in exactly the same way and does need to be an accurate fit all the way round or it will distort the shape.

LAMINATED LININGS

These can be produced from veneers if you have an excess of them. If you have a circular saw you can cut scrap timber into 1mm strips and use these. More easily, they can be readily fabricated from modeller's ply. If the ply is cut with a good sturdy craft knife across the grain it is very flexible. Two or three layers of this strip can be glued together and attached to the side (but not yet glued to it) with pegs to form it into shape. When the glue is dry the strip is taken off for trimming and sanding. Two or three layers of strip about 15mm wide make a good back lining. For front linings I recommend strips of about 7,10 and 15mm. Offcuts can be used as crossbanding, as mentioned elsewhere. This seems to me the easiest method of lining and I see no disadvantages in it.

TENTELLONES

These are small triangular blocks of wood which are glued between the front and the side after they have been glued together. They are rather like kerfed lining in appearance and effect. If you kerf a piece of rectangular section timber for kerfed linings and then cut it triangular on a band

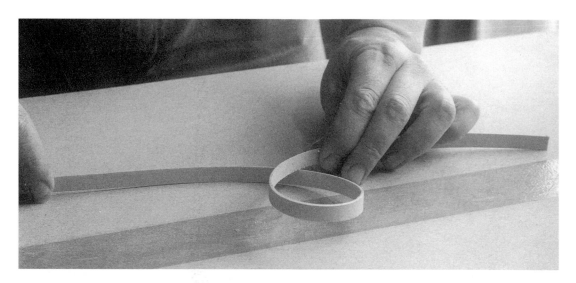

Cross-cut modeller's ply is very flexible.

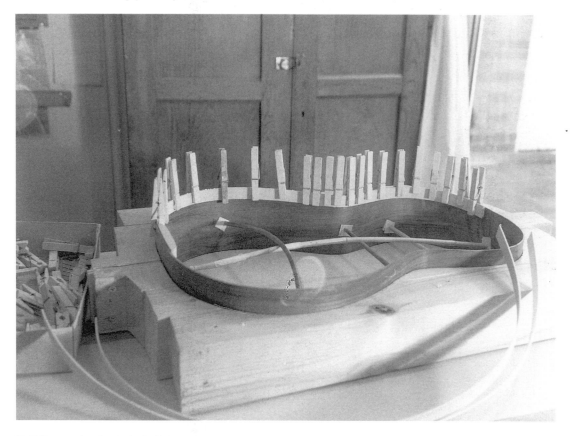

Building up laminated ply linings.

Back (left) and front (right) laminated linings in cross-section.

saw you will get an equal quantity of tentellones. They are not used on the back join.

Some people have used kerfed linings top and bottom. Others have used kerfed linings for the top but bent linings for the back, perhaps feeling that bent linings can be smooth finished more effectively as, of course, the back lining is clearly visible in the finished instrument. This combination of kerfed and bent linings is probably the commonest combination. For a really spectacular appearance the linings can be bent from the same timber as the back crossbars and the crossbanding in colour contrast with the back and sides.

10 The Assembly Procedure

The first assembly stage is to join the sides at the bottom joint with a bottom block. Almost any timber can be used that is not too dense. I have used an offcut from the mould. The grain should run parallel with the grain in the sides. The length is 100–120mm. The block needs to be a fraction wider than the sides so that trimming flush can be done with a plane. The side facing into the body is to be rounded smoothly with the block 12–18mm thick. The face that will join to the sides must be carefully shaped to fit the mould with chisel paring and sanding. Check regularly in the mould itself.

Place a piece of brown plastic parcel tape over the bottom joint of the mould. (Varnishing is not sufficient as glue may be forced into the mould joint.) Glue the bottom block and press it into place, making sure that the sides are correctly lined up. This can be held against the inside of the mould with two garden canes but it will be found that the part which extends above

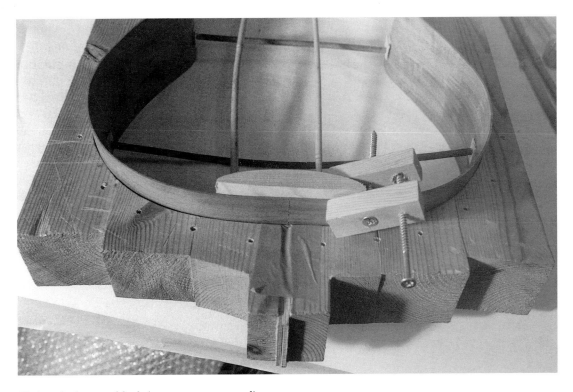

Gluing the bottom block (one cramp removed).

the mould needs cramping with large pegs or screwcramps.

The sides can be marked where they will fit into the neck joint. The distance between centre line and the ends of the wedge cut-outs top and bottom on the neck piece should be transferred to the sides, making sure that there is no confusion between front and back surfaces of the finished instrument. Once the bottom block is glued in, the sides can be removed and the marked waste sawn off. It is worth chisel cutting the ends of the sides to an angle to fit into the wedge cut-outs more neatly.

At this stage, the mould needs to have its neck sections removed and to be placed and screwed on to its backboard.

NECK GEOMETRY

Before going further we need some means of checking that the neck will lie at the correct angle to ensure that the string height above the fretboard can be adjusted satisfactorily. The backboard will be in the same plane as the perimeter of the front of the instrument, but in what plane should the front of the neck lie?

To find this out, I suggest another drawing board exercise. Draw a horizontal line across a piece of paper; this represents the plane of the front of the body. Draw a dot marking each end of the line; one represents the nut and the other the bridge saddle. The distances between the points does not matter. Now draw a dot at exactly half distance; the twelfth fret. With a straight edge and two rulers measure the front dome height. If you have made and used the strutting platen correctly it should be 3–4mm. Enter this as a faint line the said distance above your bridge end dot. On top of this, add the thickness you intend your bridge to be (perhaps 8–9mm for a start) and a couple of millimetres for a bridge saddle. Now at the other end mark the thickness you intend the nut end of the fingerboard to be (probably about 7mm). Above this mark 1.5mm to represent the string height above the fingerboard at the nut. Now mark the thickness of the fingerboard in at the twelfth fret (could be 7mm or less). Mark a dot 1mm higher to represent the thickness of fret twelve. A straight-edge placed across the two ends of this drawing should show you the predicted string height at fret twelve. There are, of course, some approximations in this and there is much adjustment that can be made when stringing the actual instrument but this drawing should be the first check on what structural adjustments are necessary. The sixth string should have a clear space above fret twelve of 3–4mm

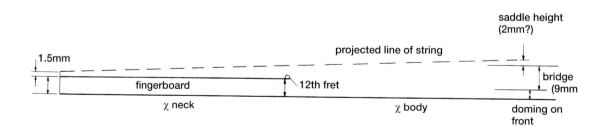

Fig 13 String height and neck geometry.

for a student instrument and 4.5–5mm for a concert instrument. The first string should be 2.5–3mm and/or 3–3.5mm respectively.

You should be able to see whether these values can be achieved on your drawing or not. If they can, this means that the neck can be joined on in the plane of the front perimeter, i.e. flat on the backboard. If not, you can play around with your drawing and change any of the parameters you set up in drawing it. Perhaps a slightly different taper to the fingerboard would be better? I tend to find that I can usually proceed to join the neck in this same plane (much the easiest way, of course) if I have about this 3–4mm dome on the front. Draw your own planned instrument and play around with its heights on paper.

If you need to put the neck in behind the plane of the front you simply block it up by the required amount (it should be no more than 1–1.5mm) with shims at the nut level during the assembly procedures. If you made a flat fronted instrument, as well as needing thicker fan strutting as explained previously, you would need to angle the neck to about 3mm above the front plane and this is more difficult. A 3mm thick mask for the inner edge of the backboard inside the mould would be necessary. But this would also require cutting the neck joint at a slight but critical angle. Any departure from the suggested setting of the neck plane with the front can complicate the fitting of the fretboard across the angle between the two as well. These are the reasons why the doming platen is so useful both to the acoustics and the logistics.

FIXING NECK TO SIDES

Ensure that the front will drop into place inside the mould and that the centre lines are correct at both ends. If the fit is a bit tight in places, trim the front carefully with a sharp craft knife or coarse sanding block. Put brown parcel tape on the inside of the front where the neck timbers will touch it to prevent adherence of glue at this stage. Place the neck in position and, as necessary, trim the neck piece to the first crossbar on the front. Ensure that this is all lying flat and that the neck is entirely symmetrical between the lines drawn for the purpose on the backboard. Gently but firmly cramp the neck into this position at the edge of the backboard. The sides can be introduced into the mould and the waist and upper bout wedged in lightly with the garden canes as before. Check that the fit of the sides into the neck joints is correct and try the cut-out wedges for fit. These loose wedges will stand proud of the rest of the neck by the front thickness.

You will need to make one or two wedging cramps to hold these loose wedge joints in position as normal cramping methods are not easy to apply here. Take a block of scrap timber and drive two screws into it approximately 50mm apart. Do another at 70mm centres. With wooden wedges as used for the fan strutting, you need to position these so that wooden wedges can be driven inside the screw heads to hold the neck joint wedges in place.

Check carefully that everything fits correctly and easily and can be assembled readily. Fit the first two edge cramping strips to the mould either side of the neck to hold the sides in contact with the front in the bottom of the mould. Only very light pressure should be applied.

When you are sure that this assembly can be done without a hitch and without hurry, you are ready for the glue. A small palette knife will be found useful for spreading the glue into all the joint parts.

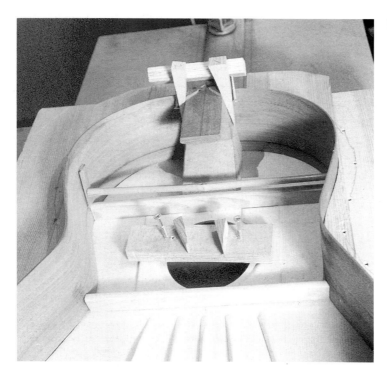

Wedging in the neck joint.

Glue between the heel and the sides and on the two inner faces of the wedges. Assemble, wedge – not forgetting to cramp the neck in alignment – and leave to dry.

FITTING LININGS

The linings are fitted at this stage. This allows them to be trimmed accurately for length at both ends, which is otherwise difficult. Glue them and fit them with a line of closely fitted pegs. Leave just enough standing proud of the sides to ensure that they can be planed down level. Plane down the bottom block and the linings where they will touch the front. Adjacent to the neck you will need to use a chisel. Angle the plane outwards by a very small amount when planing around the lower bout.

FITTING THE FRONT

Remove the protective parcel tape from the neck area of the front. Place the front in the mould and slide the neck and sides in on top of it. Lightly wedge the sides out against the mould with canes. This must not prevent the sides from moving up or down within the mould. The linings can be cut to let front crossbars in, or the crossbars can be trimmed to fit inside the linings when rib blocks will be needed. The former is normal for kerfed linings; the latter for solid linings. The neck should again be cramped symmetrically between the guide lines. Arrange every second or third of the mould surround cramping strips in place and tighten them just enough to hold the sides in contact with the front.

The cramping strips are held only by the screw through a clearance hole. This means

(*Above*) Fitting the linings.

Rib blocks.

that as they are tightened the screw may bend slightly. This is a useful reminder that only light cramping pressure is applied. Too much pressure could do untold damage. If it is really necessary to apply a little more pressure, then a small wooden block can be put under the free end of the strip. A piece of the scrap from cutting the cramping strips is ideal. In any case, some of these blocks will be necessary to the fitting of the back.

When you are confident that this all fits correctly, and without haste, loosen off the cramps. Most of them will drop out when turned parallel with the sides. Lightly run a pencil line around the inner edge of the linings and raise the sides in the mould. This should reveal a marked area where the glue must be put. Glue also the area making contact with the neck continuation and, if contact is close enough, the end of the neck where it joins the first crossbar. Reassemble without delay and lightly close up the screwcramps around the edge. Rib blocks may be added at this stage and taped until the glue dries.

FITTING THE BACK

Remove all screwcramps from the mould and lay the back on to the sides. Initially they will not fit because the inner extension of the heel is not trimmed to the first back crossbar. With the back on, reach in with a pencil and mark where it needs to be cut.

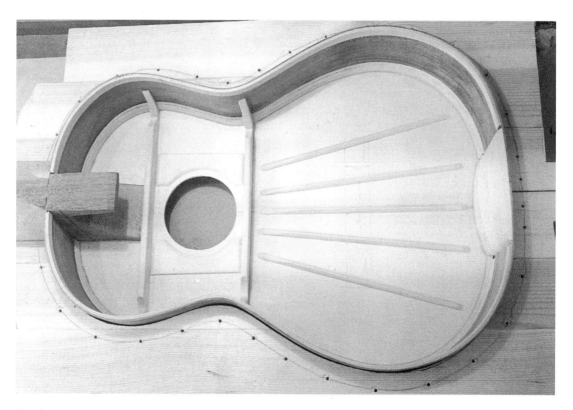

The front on.

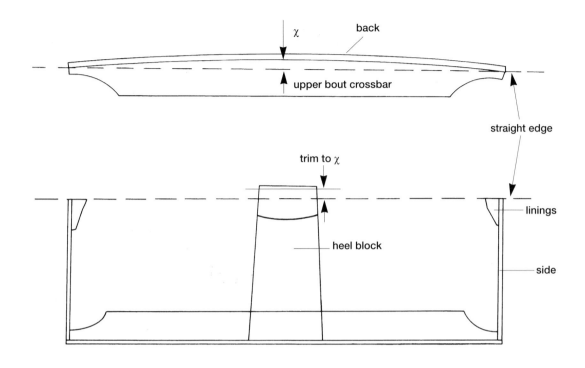

Fig 14 Fitting heel block to back curve.

When this is trimmed the back should drop into contact with the linings. These also need to be trimmed. Plane down the bottom block and linings flush with the sides. The heel will also need planing down to the correct level. It must make contact with the back above the first crossbar. This crossbar is curved. Lay a straight edge across the back alongside the bar and determine its curvature. It is likely that it is about 3mm higher in the middle than at the edge. The same measurement must be transferred to the inner heel end with a straight edge and a line drawn.

Planing to this line should ensure that these two surfaces just meet in the assembled instrument. Plane from this line flush to where the sides join the heel. This will be continued in a slightly downhill planed curve across the shield-shaped end of the heel.

At this stage, it is a good idea to trim the top of the back to reduce the amount of timber overhanging the upper bout and the heel. Leave just enough to be able to trim flush later. There is also a final piece of crossbanding to be fitted to the back and this is the time to do this most accurately. Measure from the freshly cut end of the heel piece to the bottom block. Mark the same measurement from the top of the first crossbar down the centre line of the back to find where this crossbanding must end if it is not to foul the bottom block.

This can now be cut and fitted as before.

The scalloped ends of the crossbars should now make contact with the back linings. Ensure that the centre line of the back is correctly positioned at the bottom block and the heel, and lightly tape in place at both ends with the first crossbar pressed against the heelpiece. With a pencil, mark a line to cut on each crossbar end where the lining joins the side. The crossbars are going to drop into slots cut into the lining but not the side. At the same time you should be able to mark where the crossbars intersect the linings ready to cut these slots. Remove the back, cut the ends of the crossbars to fit and ensure that the newly cut ends are 6mm deep. Set a marking gauge to this. Mark the linings where they are to be cut out and mark the depth inside the lining. The linings are cut with a fine saw and the waste chiselled out to the full 6mm depth.

The back should now fit on with the crossbar ends fitting their slots. Check that good contact is made between back and linings at each crossbar and at the sides of the heel. Remove the bracing canes from inside the body and re-check the fit all round.

Once again, it is a good idea at this point to do a 'dry run', fitting the back on and attaching and tightening all the cramping strips. Where the cramping strips are pressing on the short grain at the widest edges of the bouts, it is a good idea to put support blocks under the free ends to prevent the strip from pressing at an angle that may break out the grain. Be aware that overtightening is possible in this situation.

With a great deal of screw tightening to do in a limited time it helps to have a cordless screwdriver, but if one is not available a geared hand or breast drill is a good alternative with a screwdriver bit in the

Marking for cutting crossbars into the linings.

Linings cut out square and 6mm deep.

Gluing the back on. Note the use of blocks at outer edges of both bouts.

chuck. It is not a good idea to use a manual screwdriver only to find your arm seizing up with the glue going off.

When it comes to applying glue, it must be remembered that the joint you are gluing is easy to see through the hole but it is definitely not easy to clean glue from. Use just enough glue to do the job but not to run. Glue the internal heelpiece and bottom block and then run a thin line of glue round the lining surface. Do not at this stage glue the heel to the continuation of the back. Tighten cramping strips at the sides of the neck and the bottom block first and then fill in round the sides.

When the glue is thoroughly dry the cramps can be removed and the instrument removed from the mould. If this is at all stiff it is safest to remove one half of the mould from the backboard. Glue can now be inserted into the heel where the back piece is to cap it. A palette knife is best for this. A G-cramp is useful here as the joint cannot slide and there is a solid heel block to cramp it against. When leaving it to dry take care that the weight of a G-cramp does not pull it over.

The 'box' of the instrument is now assembled. It has some rough edges waiting to be trimmed and these will be dealt with before going on to do the inlay work. It is worth checking to see if the assembly has changed the amount of doming of the front and to plan adjustments in the fingerboard and/or bridge.

11 Inlay Work

The binding on the guitar is that edging strip around the front and rear perimeter of the body. Its function is said to be the sealing off of endgrain but with modern finishes I'm not sure that this still applies. Older guitars from one well known maker included a model quite without binding where the edge of the front is clearly visible and the edge of the back is only concealed by the thickness of coloured varnish.

The question is: how else would you finish the edge? It could be done with a rounded overhang as in the violoncello family and I have seen one such guitar. It can be done simply by trimming the edges of front and back flush. Neither method has serious drawbacks in function. What would be difficult would be to have the edge integral with the side as this would necessitate a completely different style of assembly with the sides going on last.

So the binding around the body is partly fashion and partly for the luthier's convenience. Whether you agree that it is a convenience when you are trying to do it remains to be seen!

Purfling is the term used for coloured strip(s) inlaid flush into any otherwise smooth surface. The rosette is an example of purfling and it can be replaced by purfling materials. The amount and complexity of purfling inlay work on a guitar can vary from none to having multiple strips between binding and body surface on all three surfaces and more on the back centre line. Purflings may also be included in head decoration.

BINDINGS

Binding material may be bought in a wide variety of coloured woods or even as plastic (where different glues are necessary). Some of the wooden binding strips are available with a line of purfling already attached and there is no doubt that this makes life easier (usually). Bindings can be cut from timbers of your own choice if you have a circular saw. They can even be taken from the edge of the side itself although this requires some different techniques during assembly and I shall therefore deal with this technique, which I call 'self binding', separately. Binding depths vary from 3–4mm to 7–8mm and thicknesses from 1.5 up to about 3mm. I shall suggest 7mm × 2mm which would be finished off 6mm × 1.8mm approx. This is about normal but can be varied if you choose.

First, it is necessary to trim the edges of the front and back all round so that there is absolutely no overhang. This is usually done with a chisel and a cabinet scraper, taking great care to work with the grain. Where the piece of back covers the heel, it is best dealt with using the tool with which you finished off the heel itself. The marking out is a job for the adjustable inlay cutter. Use a blade made of a jigsaw blade as described in the chapter. When setting this into the arm of the cutter allow the wooden block behind the blade to drop down a little to give extra support to the blade and prevent it deflecting away from the cutter body. Set it flat side away from the body with the cutter edge 1.8mm from the body and go round the edge of the front, lightly marking from the edges of the bouts 'downhill' towards waist and end. Repeat this on the back. This should be clearly marked and incised but you are not trying to cut down into the timber at this stage.

Now set the blade to 6mm. You may prefer to switch to the flat side of the cutter body which the design in Chapter 2 allows you to do. Mark this with a clear incised cut all round the sides, front and back. These incised marks are to be deepened and extended at the neck end where the inlay cutter cannot reach, with a heavy duty craft knife. Angle the knife so that one of its honed edges is upright in the cut, otherwise you will widen the carefully measured dimension and put a sloped edge on the cut.

It is also useful to 'cut backwards'. (A confusing term; I wish I could think of a better one). What this means is to cut the last 50mm or so of the line and then to go back and cut the previous 50mm and thus to cut in short sections into a part where you have already completed the cut. Great care and the most gradual increase in the depth of cut is needed as you approach the waist point from both directions.

With every part of the cut cleanly incised, the waste has to be removed with a chisel. Take great care to work with the grain to avoid break out. Absolutely flat and clean edges to the rebate are essential for accurate work without gaps.

It is tempting to think that such rebate work ought to be possible with a router. Unfortunately, the domestic router is a rather large and heavy beast and it proves very difficult to design and build a fence of sufficient accuracy and use it effectively. Some makers have used the lighter and

Chiselling out the binding rebate working with the grain.

more specialized 'laminate trimmer' router for this but it is expensive and of limited application. Dremel have made a modeller's router to which Waverley have added a very specialized set of router fences and this is effective (if noisy at 37,000 rpm!) but one needs to be in regular production to warrant one.

It is now possible to shape and fit the bindings. If this is done accurately it is not essential to use any purfling, although it would be normal at least around the front. If you are intending purfling work you must plan ahead at this stage and know what methods you want to use. It is possible to cut out a channel for the purfling around the front edge so that you have a double step rebate: one for the purfling and one for the binding. Many people do this and some of the existing literature will tell you to do this. I do not recommend it but it is an option.

If you wish to fit a separate purfling between side and binding, I recommend that you act before attaching the bindings as I explain below.

The bindings will probably need to be pre-bent on the heating iron to some extent as it can be difficult to conceal cracks caused by incautious bending. The waist position should be found on the binding strip and bent first. Be aware that if it is one with purfling already attached this may detach if overheated. The waist should be bent fairly accurately. Ensure that there is a clear channel into which binding fits between neck and body. It needs to go about 6mm in from the edge of the neck.

There are two clear choices of glue when fitting the bindings. Bindings can be fitted

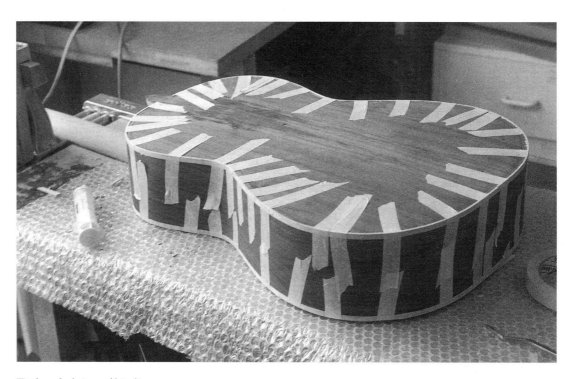

Titebond gluing of bindings.

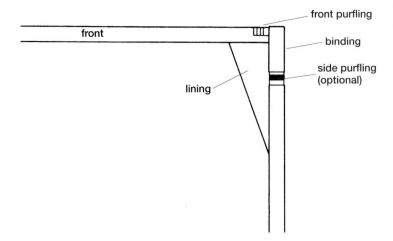

front purfling

binding

side purfling
(optional)

front

lining

Fig 15 Purfling and binding in
section.

with Titebond, holding with masking tape.
Use the slight elasticity of the tape to exert
a pressure on the bindings. Leave an hour
to harden.

More quickly, if slightly more tricky, they
can be attached with a gel-type cyanoacrylate and hardener. Put the gel in the rebate
and paint the binding with hardener. Work
no more than 150mm sections at a time
and, wearing polythene gloves, hold the
bindings in place for the 25 seconds or so
that it takes for the glue to set.

Whichever glue method you use, start at
the waist and work toward the neck, trimming to length in good time to ensure that
the neck end piece will go in vertically.
Work round the lower bout until you can
trim the piece to length at the centre line
just before gluing it. Care will be needed
with the second binding to get good central contact.

The heel end of the back binding will
need planning. The simplest perfectly neat
method is to end the bindings straight at
the sides of the heel. Alternatively, they
can be cut across the heel and joined up.
You may choose to trim the back straight
across the heel without an overhang of

back material and to cap the heel later, possibly with a fingerboard off-cut.

PURFLING

If you plan a separate purfling line
between side and binding, rather than trying to cut a channel for it I suggest that you
leave a space for it to drop into. With a
sharp craft knife cut from your purfling a
number of very short sections probably
not more than 2.5mm long. You will need
fifteen or so of these each side and you
need to ensure that you have enough purfling left when these are cut. If your purfling should be 1.5mm wide you can
substitute modeller's ply. Go round your
binding rebate and, with a single tiny drop
of Titebond on each, stick them on at
50–60mm intervals. These will space out
your bindings when you fit them. They
will then come out with a small purfling
chisel (or a watchmaker's screwdriver)
leaving a neat and accurate purfling channel. The width of this purfling will need to
have been taken into account when cutting
out for the bindings in this method.

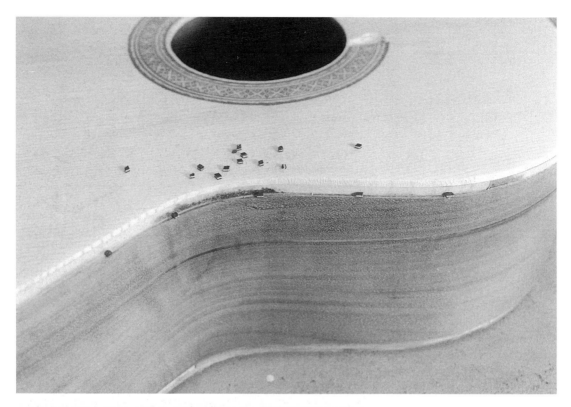

Pieces of purfling stuck on …

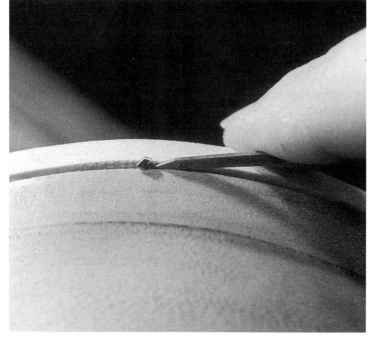

… are removed after binding fitting.

Side purfling needs to be as deep as your binding at least, i.e. 2mm so that it does not sink below the level of the sides. I recommend that you start by bending the waist. Make a bending template with a piece of modeller's ply cut out to the approximate profile of your waist and stuck down to a baseboard with non-heat-sensitive glue. With a flat iron at a high heat setting you can gradually coax the purfling round this curve to form the waist. I have never found it necessary to bend the rest.

To put Titebond into purfling channels I use a wide-bore veterinary hypodermic needle on my glue syringe. This is so much neater than other methods of application.

Start at the waist and push the purfling into its channel with a smooth piece of wood. I use a varnished chisel handle which cleans easily afterwards.

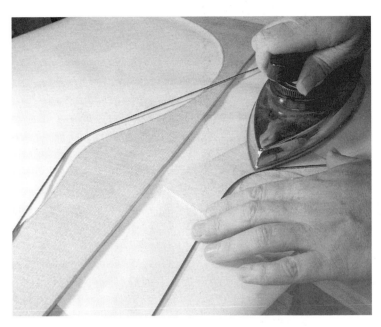

(*Above*) Pre-bending side purfling to the waist.

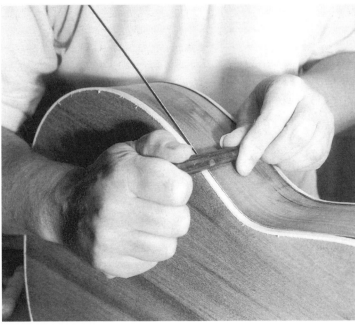

Pressing purfling into the channels.

Cutting purfling channels with the inlay cutter …

… or with a scalpel. Note the use of three purfling strips.

Work toward the neck and ensure that the end is trimmed so that it will push into its channel before the last part is pushed in. At the bottom end no very accurate trimming is needed as the end will be cut by the bottom inlay.

With the bindings already in place, there are two methods of marking out a purfling channel on the front. You can use the inlay cutter set to your purfling width plus 2mm for the binding. Alternatively, as the binding is standing about 1mm proud of the surface, it is possible to hold a piece of the purfling in place on the inside edge of the binding and to go round it with a scalpel. Be aware that it is possible, by cutting an overwide purfling in too deeply, to detach the front from the linings!

Incise the channel as before and cut the waste out with a purfling chisel. A 1.5mm depth of channel is sufficient.

Again, the needle, if you have one will deliver glue most cleanly and a varnished tool handle is the ideal pressing tool. You may feel that masking tape is necessary to hold it down while glue dries. Take great care to finish the purfling strips on the centre line or, if you prefer they can be

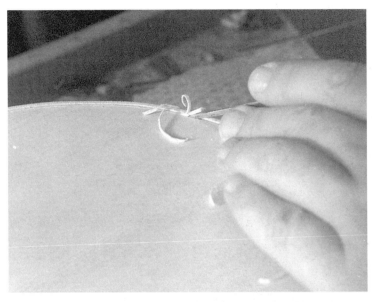

(*Above*) Chiselling out for purfling.

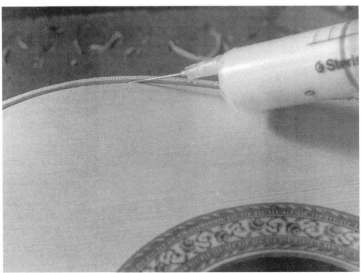

Gluing with a syringe needle is neater.

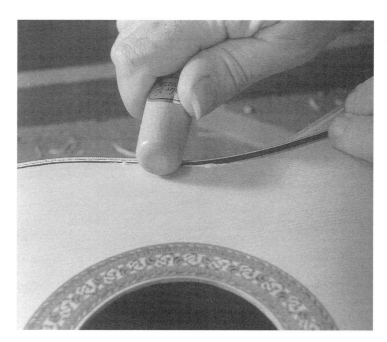

Pressing the purfling into place: a single layer in this photograph.

scarfed somewhere just off centre to hide the join. Edge purfling the back is essentially identical to the front.

It is necessary to cut an inlay piece to cover the joint between the sides at the bottom. This can be of binding material or some other, usually contrasting piece. The piece should be cut to size to fit accurately between the bindings and can be held in place while its outline is incised across the join. Ensure that this is central. The channel for this should be chiselled out to less than the depth of the piece so that it can be finished back flush. If there is side purfling fitted it is normal to continue this down the sides of the end inlay. Cut out for this purfling around the bottom inlay with the inlay still standing proud of the sides and a piece of purfling held in place. Careful mitring is necessary in the corners to give continuity to the purfling colours.

Back inlay is another possibility. Full decoration of a guitar includes purfling layers down the back, on or near the centre line and joining up with the edge purfling in some way. I prefer to make a good bookmatch join in the back and leave it to speak for itself but the technique is straightforward. A good straight-edge longer than the back is necessary and double-sided tape is really useful. Make the cuts one at a time and only after drawing them on in sharp pencil first. Mark them with the craft knife working against the straight-edge, held down very firmly (if the straight-edge slips it can be a bit terminal!). When channels have been incised on both sides, cut out the waste with a purfling or carver's dog-leg chisel to no more than 1mm (remembering that the back is not much more than 2mm thick). Gluing and purfling application is as before. Where back inlays do not fall within the area covered on the other side by the crossbanding, they weaken the back and increase the likelihood of a split developing.

(*Above*) Cutting the bottom inlay.

Mitring in purfling at the bottom.
Note the use of a burnished knife
blade to get 45 degrees easily.

Variation in design of bottom inlay.

SELF BINDING

This is a rather different technique which includes differences at the stage of assembling the box of the guitar. It consists of bending the sides as before and then marking and cutting the future bindings from the edge of the side. Where you have a timber with grain pattern features that run across the grain such as flamed Maple, bird's eye Maple or nicely quilted Mahogany, for example, these features can run from front to back and continue through the side puflings (which are essential in this case). The sides are probably best left 2mm thick for this method.

Cutting the edges from the sides can be done with the inlay cutter against a rounded wooden 'anvil' or with a Japanese saw blade of very small kerf. I have set up a purpose-built table to my motorized fretsaw for this operation. Each edge binding should be pencil marked for identification before cutting.

If the side were cut out to recieve this binding, continuity of grain pattern would be lost so the rebate for the bindings must be left at the construction stage. The internal linings must be attached to the side with enough standing proud of the side to create the rebate. To do this accurately for the front involves fitting the linings before

Self-binding. Grain is continuous from side into binding.

Fig 16 Planning 'self' bindings.

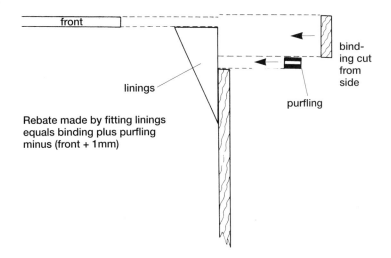

front

linings

binding cut from side

purfling

Rebate made by fitting linings
equals binding plus purfling
minus (front + 1mm)

attaching the sides to the neck. The lining is then planed back to a level where the remaining rebate plus the thickness of front or back at this point on the body adds up to 6mm (plus the side purfling thickness). The thickness of the back may be constant but the thickness of the front probably is not, so some meticulous measurement is needed. This requires careful planning as well as careful planing!

While on this subject of cutting from the side, if you produce guitars in more than one colour of timber you can have a constant cheap supply of contrasting bindings by cutting them all 14mm too wide and cutting the edges back to correct dimension.

For the beginner I would not recommend this latter technique. I would suggest that if the bindings can be fitted sufficiently accurately so that no gaps are left between back binding and back timber no purfling is necessary there. With carefully chosen contrast bindings, side purfling is a luxury and only the front needs a simple purfling line. I do recommend that

you buy ready made purfling in wood. Good purfling is made from non-porous timbers and will remain clean when sanded. Any porous timbers in the guitar's decoration is in danger of looking scruffy if it can absorb dust from another timber.

However, it is possible to create your own designs of purfling if you have the necessary veneers. What is needed is a piece of sheet timber (MDF is best) with the shape of the side of your guitar cut out from it. Tack a line of small nails in both sides, spacing them alternately. Varnish the edge. Next cut a piece of modeller's ply to fit this edge and varnish one side of it. The purfling veneers should be cut out with the modeller's ply as template. After gluing, they are mounted on the edge, covered by the ply and the whole sandwich is held in place with string windings around the nails. When it is dry the strip has to be edged and cut into widths suitable for purfling.

Purfling and binding is taken down to flush with the surfaces using a cabinet

103

scraper. This can be long and a bit tedious as a job but there are no shortcuts that I can recommend. Cutting tools are very likely to cause damage. In scraping the front and back the you must work with the grain of the binding but control the curvature of the scraper so that the face is not touched until it is very nearly flush. The final finish is with abrasive sheet but do not leave yourself a lot of binding to sand off.

Scraping bindings, keeping them level with the side.

(*Below*) Scraping purflings. Bend scraper away from softwood fronts.

12   The Fingerboard

The fingerboard is made of a hard and close-grained timber and the most popular for high-quality guitars has become Ebony. However, I explained in Chapter 3 on Timbers why I would not recommend Ebony for a first instrument and why Rosewood is probably better. You will need a piece about 500mm long and at least 70mm wide. You must be able to plane it to get a good even 7mm thickness. Mark a chosen face surface and then plane the back absolutely flat. Plane one side square and straight.

The top of the fingerboard by the nut could be anything between 50mm (small) and 56mm (very large). The top of the front of the neck should have lines down it at either 50mm or 52mm width but some waste (1mm or so) either side of this. Let us suggest a fingerboard of 54mm at this end. At the neck – body junction the width should be about 62mm and the lines drawn on the neck should be this spacing. Mark these dimensions on the fingerboard material with the 54mm about 10mm from one end and the 62mm at the level of the junction (325mm further down). Continuing these two points as a straight line, cut and plane square to the line.

It is necessary to have an adjustable sliding bevel or other tool which can be set up and locked to an angle near to 90 degrees. Set up the angle so that the blade of the bevel follows the same light pencil line across the timber when used from either side. This is a line at right angles to the centre of the fingerboard and can be used to mark the nut end at the level where 54mm is marked. Cut this across with a fine-toothed tenon saw. Preserve this angle on the bevel for fret cutting later.

Put the fingerboard in place on the neck and line it up centrally and accurately at the nut. Mark a line where the hole comes so that it can be roughly trimmed to reduce overhang and remove the waste. Then line it up again and tape it firmly into position on the neck. A suitable scriber can be made from a sharpened nail and a piece of hard-wood scrap, and used to mark the position of the hole on the fingerboard underside. If everything is central the mark at each side should match up with the bevel placed across.With a fret saw or coping saw cut to the line, leaving an absolute minimum to be sanded off later.

At or about this stage it is a good idea to make something to keep working detritus out of the body of the instrument. My own device is rather like a very small fez hat made of 12mm upholstery foam put together with contact adhesive. Its brim width is slightly wider than the hole and its height is slightly more than the depth of a guitar. It can be crushed in one hand and put in through the hole where it springs back into shape on the underside.

To glue the fingerboard in place you will need two of the smallest-sized screwcramps and four of the specially designed screwcramps detailed in the Tools chapter with their balsa-wood pads in place. Place them over the fingerboard and check that they all fit well. Adjust the small screwcramps to

Gluing on the fingerboard.

hold the fingerboard down on the edge of the hole. Check that the fingerboard does fit down especially where a square steel tube has been routed and glued. Scrape off any traces of epoxy if necessary.

Apply Titebond to the fingerboard underside sparingly but evenly and place it down on the neck. Fix the small screw-cramps from inside the hole and ensure correct placing. Slide all four screwcramps on to the neck and tighten the nut end one first. Keep the jaws as parallel as possible by even tightening. Check the positioning carefully as you tighten up. Fix a G-cramp from the back of the heel to the finger-board over the body taking care not to overtighten. Take care where you leave the

instrument to dry so that the weight of the G-cramp is not in danger of pulling it over. This should be left overnight.

With the cramps off, the shaping of the neck can be finished. If only the very edge of the neck has been left it should be a job for the cabinet scraper. If you have been a little more 'shy' of the very edge, you may need a stroke or two with the spokeshave again. To get a really neat flush finish you need to take scraper shavings which include neck timber and the fingerboard all the way down. This should leave the planed sides of the fingerboard untouched along the front edge.

The front of the fingerboard should now be planed. If you do not have a vice which

Finishing the neck – fingerboard joint flush.

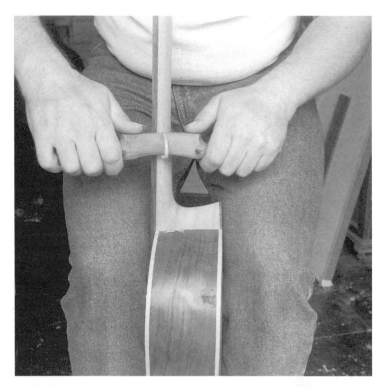

Blending into the heel.

makes this easy, you will need to arrange a block of wood, cramped to the bench with a step in it at the right height to hold the head. The head can be held in place with a strip of wood and two screws through the stringslots.

It is also advisable to make an upper bout guard. Cut a piece of modeller's ply to cover the width of the upper bout, down to near the bridge position and cut out a section so that it drops over the fingerboard. A couple of strips of small section wood can be glued on in such a way that they locate above the upper bout alongside the neck.

Plane the front of the fingerboard flat. The thickness at the nut and at fret twelve should already have been decided upon when you drew up plans for the neck setting in Chapter 10. Check by looking back at your drawing. The fingerboard for your first guitar should be flat and of identical thickness on both sides. If you have decided to taper it check the dimensions and the flatness regularly. If it gets too thin over the body, fret cutting will be difficult.

FRET POSITIONING

Now you are in a position to start thinking where the frets go. You should have a distance of 325mm between the start of the fingerboard and the point where the neck joins the body.

Let us take the normal standard 'scale length' of 650mm. When this is vibrating over its whole length it produces a note caused by the vibration of air of x vibrations per second. If it is then stopped at half distance (fret twelve) it will provide vibrations

Planing the fingerboard.

of 2x vibrations per second and we hear a note one octave higher. In terms of the music made on the guitar, each octave is divided into twelve equal parts which make the chromatic scale. So we need to produce twelve equally spaced notes. Unfortunately, this does not mean that the frets are equally spaced. Frets are so spaced that each fret shortens the string length by exactly the same proportion as the previous fret and that the twelfth fret achieves half the original string length. Summed up in mathematical terms, this means that each fret is the twelfth root of two further along the string. This is resolved in practical terms by a number which we can use to calculate fret positions.

If you take the scale length and divide it by 1.0594631 (assuming an 8-position calculator) you will get the vibrating length of the string when stopped at its next fret.

650mm ÷ 1.0594631 = 613.51829mm
fret 2 " = 579.08415
fret 3 " = 546.58265
fret 4 " = 515.90532

The rest of the positions can be had by simply pressing the '=' on the calculator.

If you take the scale length and divide it by 17.817151 you will get the position of the next fret.

650mm ÷ 17.817151 = 36.481702mm.

This then has to be subtracted from the 650mm and the calculation repeated. This takes slightly longer unless you have a programmable calculator.

Both of these methods produce the same result and can be checked by their producing the twelfth fret at half the scale length (note also that 613.51829 and 36.481702 add up to 650).

One of the first things to point out is that accuracies of better than 0.5mm are inappropriate to pencil marking and saw cutting. Round all such values to the nearest half millimetre. Calculate all the fret positions you need and check fret twelve before rounding the decimals or marking the fingerboard.

These are the principles on which fret positions are calculated and you should be able to use them to calculate the fret positions for any scale length and for any number of frets. If you have stuck to the standard scale length of 650mm then I can supply the fret positions:

fret	position (mm)	
1	36.5	
2	71	
3	103.5	
4	134	
5	163	
6	190.5	
7	216	
8	240.5	
9	263.5	
10	285	
11	305.5	
12	325	
13	343	
14	360.5	
15	377	
16	392	
17	406.5	
18	420	
19	433	traditionally the last fret
20	445.5	(needed for some pieces of music)

These figures are written on my workshop wall. I prefer working with zero on the ruler at the nut end so these figures were

109

calculated using 17.82. The approximation causes an error of less than the thickness of a pencil line by the end of the fingerboard.

COMPENSATION

When you push a string down to its fret the action of your finger increases the tension in the string and this raises the pitch of the note produced. Therefore, if you fitted the frets so that fret twelve was at 325mm and the string length was actually 650mm then your octave note would sound sharp i.e. at too high a pitch. The only way to correct this is to make the remaining string length a fraction too long. This is done in the positioning of the bridge so that the string saddle in the bridge actually stops the strings at more than 650mm. Thus the notional string length or scale length is 650mm and is essential for planning the fret positions. The actual full length of the open vibrating string is more by some millimetres. The actual position of the bridge saddle is not something that one can be totally precise about.

Not all strings behave in exactly the same way. Thicker strings require greater compensation. No one compensation setting can be right for strings E, B and G. Similarly, D, A and bass E each require a little more for accurate pitch. Naturally, higher string action in terms of the distance between the strings and the twelfth fret also changes the compensation needed for correct pitch. So what we need is a best approximation instead of a correct answer. It also helps if we leave ourselves room for late adjustments and to this end I recommend (in the next chapter) a wider bridge saddle than was traditional.

I have read that the string length should be scale length plus 2mm, but I consider

2mm is inadequate. In my experience, working approximations of effective compensations are as follows:

Treble	E	2.5mm
	B	3.0
	G	4.0
	D	3.0
	A	3.5
Bass	E	4.0

I shall not enter the debate as to whether compensation should all be added to the bridge end of the string or whether some portion of it should be taken off at the nut end; I merely note its existence.

Once you have decided what your fret positions are they should be marked down the centre of the fingerboard with a pencil or craft knife. Then with your sliding bevel lightly mark one of them across in pencil and re-check that the bevel is giving you the same reading from either side. When you are satisfied mark the fret positions down as far as you can. When you get to the fingerboard over the body you need to turn the bevel over and use the other end of it or adjust its setting so that it can be used the other way round.

When all your fret positions are marked you are ready to saw the grooves that the frets will fit into. This requires a saw with a kerf of a rather exact width. The saw kerf needs to be 0.56mm. Such saws can be bought sized ready for use but it is possible to reduce the kerf of a gent's-type saw yourself by rubbing it on an oilstone on both sides until it is right. A micrometer is really useful here. If the frets are forced into too small a slot you will induce a convex curve in the fingerboard and this cannot be made to give a playable action. It is vital to get the fret slots sawn to the correct width.

Marking fret positions …

… and scribing them across.

Sawing fret kerfs.

Before sawing measure the depth of the 'tang' – the vertical section of your fretwire and mark with a pencil in your inlay cutter to this depth (a bit of 1.5 ply may be needed taped to the body to get this setting). When cutting the fret slots it is very important to keep the saw vertical as the fretwire will not bend to accommodate inaccuracies in this plane. Try to saw the slot in one go. Every time the saw is taken in and out of the cut the slot gets a little wider. Good lighting is critical. Cut just through the pencil guide line by an absolute minimum amount and ensure that the saw blade can be let down to the lines on both sides. This will ensure that the bottom of the slot is flat. When you get near to the body put the upper bout guard in place.

In my experience, saws with depth stops on them designed to be set to the fret-tang depth are not a good idea. They tend to leave marks on the fingerboard and can also obscure your view of the line you are trying to cut to.

FRETWIRE

There is a good variety of shapes and sizes of fretwire available from suppliers as they are intended for use on a variety of sizes and styles of instrument. Tiny fretwire can be had for mandolins and some rather enormous stuff is available for such as acoustic bass guitars along with most sizes in between. Traditionally, guitar fretwire was quite small and low and the justification for this was that it facilitated sliding the fingers along the fingerboard when necessary and, in any case, it preserved accurate intonation. But it made barré work a nightmare for some students as the left index finger is nobody's idea of a good straight-edge. Proponents of it seemed to think that it forced the player to strive for good technique. There is a move more recently toward the acceptance of larger fretwire for its greater ease of playing cleanly. Greater increase of tension in pushing the string down between deeper frets changes intonation, it can be argued; but this can be taken into account in setting the compensation is the reply. Some makers have recently introduced differently structured fret materials of effectively much larger section.

So traditionally the fretwire would have been about 2mm wide and would finish less than 1mm high. Larger fretwire up to perhaps 2.8mm is now acceptable and this tends to finish about 1.30mm high. It isn't a big difference to look at but the feel of the instrument in the hands cannot fail to be noticed.

Fretwire is not all made of the same alloy. The softest can be bent easily by the fingers and is said to make fret fitting much easier. Unfortunately, its wear properties are softer too and it does not retain such a polished appearance, so I cannot recommend anything that is not clearly labelled 'Hard'. The specification 18 per cent nickel silver ensures good quality fretwire.

The hammer required to insert the frets needs to be smoothly finished to a slight dome with the edges of the face rounded off. Mine is 26mm across the face and weighs 330g. It could be a little larger, but not much.

Before starting, you will also need a block to support the back of the neck. This should be surfaced with leather or balsa-wood to prevent marking it and should support the neck horizontally with the instrument lying on some support sheet, probably bubble plastic. You will also need stout wire cutters capable of cutting almost flush to an edge.

Your fretwire may be in the form of a roll. If so, it can be looped around the neck at the end of the bench at least for the first half of

Fretwire is a press fit, hammered in …

... and nipped off nearly flush.

the fingerboard. This should allow one end to be pulled into position over the fretslot.

Trim one end of the wire as cleanly as you can with your cutters and present it with only the very slightest overhang on one end of the first slot. With support block in place, hammer it into the slot, checking that it stays upright and work along the width of the fingerboard until the end is in. At this point, cut it off as clean and close as you can before checking along the length and tapping in wherever you can see space between the fretwire and the timber. It is likely that the first end may have lifted slightly. Retrim the new end of the next fret before insertion.

Once you get to the body you will probably want to cut each fret to approximate length and place them individually. It can be more difficult to cut them off closely over the body but this will be done by edge filing. The fact that, in the design I have suggested, the neck block continues to the first cross strut is of use here. It gives more support to the fingerboard over the body when hammering frets in. A block of dense hardwood will be needed for hammering in the eighteenth and, if fitted, the split nineteenth frets. It is held inside the hole against the underside of the front. In the traditional design without continued neck block this is needed for all the body frets.

If you do find a fret will not go all the way in, you should assume that the hole is incorrectly cut. Remove and recut. If it goes in but will not stay down, the hole may have been cut or have become too wide. For the remedy, see the following section.

When all frets are in to your satisfaction the ends need filing off. With the upper bout guard in place, take a file blade and run it along the edge of all the frets until almost flush with the woodwork; then angle the file in toward the fingerboard by a small amount – perhaps 10 degrees – and finish filing flush. This will take a tiny chamfer off the top edge of the fingerboard. Your scraper took a slight cut out of the

Edge filing frets.

bottom of the planed fingerboard side. This file cut will do the same to the top edge and lead, after sanding, to a nice subtle slight roundness to the whole edge. The file cut should be continued down the treble side of the fingerboard at about 30 degrees or so but this cut should stop short of touching the woodwork and is intended only to cut back the frets where the left-hand fingers will run up and down the neck.

REFRETTING

Frets do wear down so one of the luthier's regular tasks is refretting an older instrument. The first job is removing the old frets. This is done with a chisel ground to a single bevel, and a piece of drinks can. Using the metal sheet under the chisel at all times, one corner of the fret is lifted. As

soon as sufficient has been lifted to get the chisel in, it is inserted straight on under the fret and wriggled from side to side as it is pushed forward. Putting new frets in is identical to the procedure for fitting frets from new except that you may find that the fretslots are worn and a loose fit.

Whenever the slot is too big it can be lined with glue. The idea is to run glue into the slot and leave it to dry. This puts a new hard lining in the slot and allows a new fretslot to be cut by the normal method. It is important that frets are mounted only in dry glue since, if the frets were adhering to their surrounding wood the surface of the fingerboard would come away with the frets when next removed and this can be extremely difficult for the next luthier.

Bound fingerboards present another slight problem. The tang of the fret needs to be taken off back to the thickness of the binding. There are wirecutters designed to do this but it can be done with a well designed holding block and a file.

Recutting fretslots on a bound fingerboard necessitates the removal of the binding or the making of a special fretting saw.

Lifting ...

... and removing frets.

13   The Bridge

The bridge is the most massive of the pieces of wood glued to the front of your guitar. In weight it probably equals all the fan struts put together. We must therefore conclude that it is of major acoustic significance as well as being one of the most visible pieces of your instrument. Great care therefore is put into building it and fitting it. Care has already been put into its relationship with the fan strutting.

The front has a dome built into it for good acoustic reasons and the bridge is to become an integral part of this. It is therefore essential that the bridge fits the front. In order to get a perfect fit between bridge and front it is a good idea to start with an oversized block of timber, since producing an accurate concave surface to fit the convex front needs firm holding in a vice. The best timber is probably the timber you use for the fingerboard as it holds the colour co-ordination together well. Similar timbers are suitable if they are not too dense. Your best starting point might be a small turnery blank. My suggested design of bridge is 175mm long and 28–29mm wide. It ends up about 9mm thick but this is hardly enough to start with. A starting piece 30mm square by 200mm long is about right.

This has to be held in a vice, bottom side up and planed concave in the middle as far as your plane allows. Try this on your

Scraping the bridge underside …

... to fit the guitar front.

guitar front. Further material is taken off with the cabinet scraper. This has the advantage that it will allow you to get a slightly concave surface on your bridge in cross-section, too. It is difficult to work across the start and finish of a piece of timber with a scraper so this is why your blank is at least 15mm too long to start with; the ends can be discarded later. Work carefully and methodically with the scraper and try the bridge blank against the front frequently. When you get somewhere near a fit, it will be necessary to designate a bass side and a treble side. Write these on the bridge. You need to get a really good fit where the bridge blank can be put down in position and no gaps are seen around the edge. You will need to pencil in lightly the position of the bridge to get it in the correct position each time.

When you are satisfied with the fit you will need to pencil in markings for the bass and treble sides of the bridge on its underside. Mark a point 9mm above the centre of the curved underside and mark it across

to an equal thickness either end. Cut and plane to this line. Mark a centre line across the top and draw in your central part and your wings in pencil.

It is advisable to drill the string holes before cutting out the central channel that they open into. This prevents the drill leaving any breakout of the surface but it means very precise drilling to bring the drill holes to the correct point. The best way to plan this is at the drawing-board.

Draw an enlarged cross-section of your bridge 9mm high by 28mm wide. One side of this is the string tie block and the other is the saddle mount. I suggest that you plan in a tie block 12mm wide with a 4.5mm channel in front of it. The string holes really ought to open into the bottom corner of this channel. Plan in on your drawing where they go and measure from your drawing how far back down the tie block they start and what angle they make.

The position of the individual holes must be planned according to the centre-line you have drawn on your bridge. They

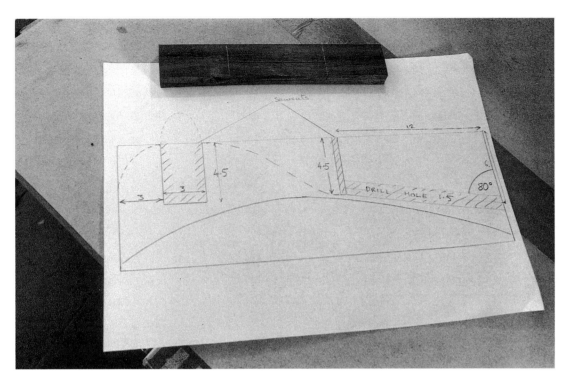

Plan the bridge at the drawing-board for accuracy.

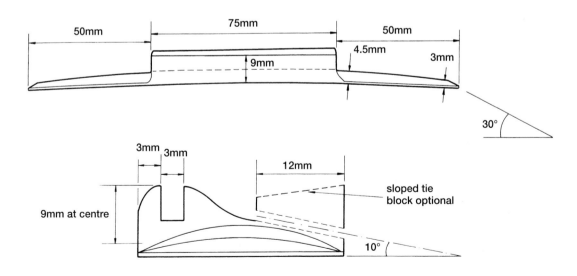

Fig 17 Suggested bridge design.

119

Drilling to a planned depth and angle …

… brings the holes out in the right place.

are normally 11.5mm apart giving a total distance Bass E to Treble E of 57.5mm. The holes are normally 1.5mm. Before drilling mark the depth of hole needed on the drill bit with a fragment of masking tape. Drill at the correct spacing, angle and depth.

The saddle slot can usually be cut at the same depth of 4.5mm. I recommend that it is 3mm wide. This is more than the traditional width but it gives you a little allowance to adjust the compensation point later and it means that a different compensation can be arranged for each string. A 3mm saddle slot should be cut 3mm in from the front edge of the bridge. Add this to your drawing.

The perfect method of cutting these two channels precisely is with a circular saw. This will allow the cuts to be made easily and with absolutely precise depth and flat-bottomed channels. A good holding push stick needs to be devised from scrap. If a circular saw is not available the most important part of this cutting is for the saddle slot bottom to be absolutely flat and square.

The shape of the saddle slot mound is established with a chisel. The front of the tie block can be removed with a chisel and planed down to slope toward the mound if you wish. Check that the holes are all showing.

Saw cuts are made to separate off the central area from the wings. This can also be at 4.5mm depth. The wings are shaped by removing the top waste with a saw and then filing to shape with the central block held in a vice. The precise depth of the wings and their contours is one of those parameters that can never be quoted exactly. It is judged according to the stiffness of the timber and its weight, and of course it is intended to match in with the thickness and stiffness of the front as well as the position and stiffness of the fan struts. So, much skilled judgement and feeling and twisting of the developing bridge may take place. However, I must give you some guidance for your first one so I suggest that the wing alongside the central block be 4–4.5mm thick and that the end of the wing, trimmed to length about this time, should be about

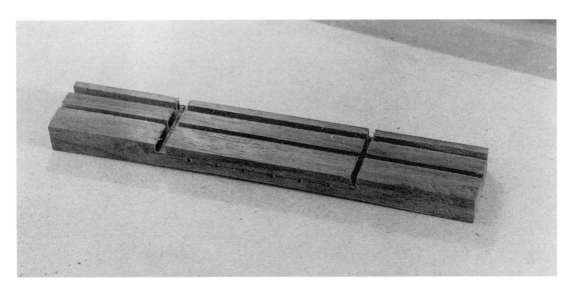

Cutting saddle slot, string channel and wings is best with a circular saw.

Filing the wings to shape.

Shaping the saddle mound.

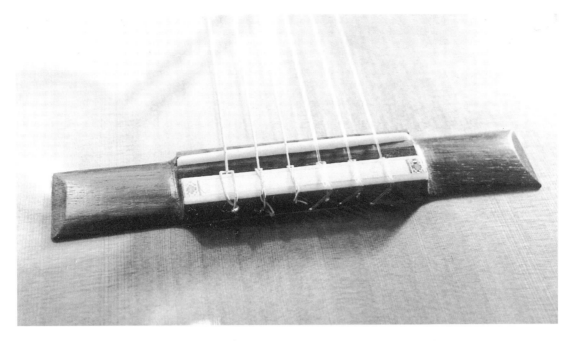

A finished bridge. Note the use of rosette fragments.

3mm before chamfering off the end at about 30 degrees. The wings do not feather off to nothing but end up 0.5–1mm thick at the perimeter.

Remove all marks and finish to a fine grade of abrasive sheet.

Precise fitting of the bridge on the front is of paramount importance. Once the front is finally finished ready for lacquer, the bridge position is marked. The bridge must be placed on the front such that a straightedge down the bass side and treble side of the fingerboard are equidistant from their respective string holes. The twelfth fret to the nearer edge of the saddle slot must be 2–2.5mm more than the nut to twelfth fret distance. When this position is established, tape down the bridge and lightly mark the position with the point of a scalpel blade held at such an angle that no markings are visible while the bridge is in place.

14 Finishing

SURFACE FINISHING

The first step in finishing is smoothing the surface with abrasive sheets. It should be worth going down to 400 grit by the usual stages and most of this is essentially like any woodwork job. The waist will need a little more attention than most areas. Also the sides of the heel are always difficult as you are sanding up to an internal corner. Smoothly join the scrapered neck side of the fingerboard with its filed front edge in a neat slight curve.

It is only at this stage that you round over the sides of the hole, after sanding the fingerboard end and its adjacent hole edge flush. Check the constancy of width of the front timber inside the rosette and round it from top and bottom.

Leave rounding the bindings until you are down to finer grades of abrasive. Material sands off corners very quickly and you can take more off more easily than you can put it back! Round the binding but none of the timber within it (i.e. radius equals binding thickness).

The guitar fine sanded. Sand the fingerboard end and nineteenth frets flush with the hole and round the hole edges.

MASKING

The next job is masking the bridge position and the fingerboard front. The bridge position is most effectively masked with Titebond. The outline of the bridge is visible as a very light scalpel scratch. Paint the area inside this thinly with the glue and let it dry. This will keep the finish material from the timber and, later, when you cut the surface finish off this area it will already be glue sized.

Mask the fingerboard with masking tape. Get the masking tape right into the corners between fingerboard and fret as there is a tendency for finish to creep alongside the fret edges by capillary attraction. Finish the masking tape to a precise craft-knife cut along the edge. Under no circumstances allow any masking tape paper to hang over the edge.

THE LACQUER

The traditional finish was French polish though this is not easy to put on the complex surfaces of a guitar. If you continue in luthiery you may need to learn French polishing for restoration work but I cannot recommend it for new instruments. It is not robust and is very susceptible to humidity and handling.

There are a number of modern lacquer finishes, some of which must be sprayed: others of which give you the option of brushing. Spray finishing can be problematic due to the amount of solvent put into the atmosphere. If it is fine summer weather you can do it successfully outside but you really need a finish you can put on any time. I have tried spraying on water emulsion acrylics and, apart from a dislike of spraying water on to carefully dried

Masking the bridge position
with glue.

Masking off the fingerboard front.

timber, I cannot tell you how to get a satisfactory finish with them.

I come down to two choices: cellulose lacquer and Rustin's Plastic Coating. I have sprayed cellulose to good effect on the instrument but not on my chest! I have brushed on both and the smell is less than spraying. If you use cellulose, ensure that it is a woodwork and not a motor-trade grade.

I do not use grain fillers as they contain pigments and are prone to stain purflings as well as masking some of the natural colour gradations in the timber. I grain fill with varnish as I shall explain.

It is a good idea to arrange a hook to hang the instrument on by its machine-head holes, in, of course, a dust-free environment.

I recommend brush application. Both materials handle in much the same way. Cellulose comes ready mixed and dries by solvent evaporation. Plastic coating has to be mixed with the hardener. It dries by solvent evaporation but then hardens by catalytic activity. Rustins, although acid catalysed, is NOT one of those that causes later refinishing problems as some are reputed to do.

Two sizes of brush are needed. You will need something like a 10mm brush for head details and a 40mm one for most of the body. Varnish brushes are available through Luthier's Supplies or large nylon water-colour brushes can be used, available from any art shop.

The front of an instrument needs a very thin layer of lacquer. Too much changes the natural properties of the timber and impairs the tone. The back and sides, however, and particularly the neck are more robust and no less effective acoustically with quite a thick layer. For these reasons, I treat the front and the rest separately.

The front can be finished with Rustins entirely by cloth if you wish to keep it really thin. I usually put a couple of layers of very slightly thinned Plastic Coating on with a cloth first with an hour to dry between (cellulose is less amenable to cloth application).

On the next day the hole can be used to hold the instrument in such a way that the whole of the rest of the surface can be brush coated. When brushing with lacquer do not wipe the brush on the jar side during use. This leads to the development of tiny granules of lacquer which cause large spots in the finish. Drain your brush over the jar until dripping stops. In warm conditions a second coat can often be given by the time you have been all the way round, and then a third. Always brush out sufficiently to avoid runs but with a minimum of strokes.

Brushes should be immersed in thinner but held off the container bottom by pegs on the handle.

After three coats it is worth cutting back with fine abrasive sheet. You will notice that the lacquer does not fill tiny holes and crevices very well. After cutting back you will find some slight crevices and the grain of porous timbers filled with a white powder of lacquer dust. If you do not remove this dust the next layer of lacquer will soak into it and reconstitute it, filling the hole slightly. This is grain filling with lacquer and the more times you do it the smoother your surface will become. You may want

an absolutely smooth, laminate-like finish and this can be obtained by repeatedly cutting back and relacquering. I prefer to leave some natural texture on timber. With this method you have complete control by how carefully you dust down and how many coats you use.

If you need to fill minor crevices around purflings there are two materials you can use. You can make up a colourless paste of lacquer and lacquer dust (you'll have a lot of this!) and put it in with a palette knife. Alternatively, epoxy resin can be used. Both must be left to harden and be smoothed down before recoating.

When you are satisfied with the back and sides, etc. the front can be finished. Lay the guitar face up and cut back lightly with a micro grade (i.e. 1500 or more) wet and dry. With slightly thinned lacquer, apply two coats by brush with an hour between. The horizontal position prevents runs in the thinned lacquer but not the sides so wipe the sides with a solvent damp cloth after every coat. If you prefer cloth coating the front it will take four or five layers of this.

Once this is done, you must leave the instrument for several days for hardening to take place.

FLATTING AND BUFFING

You will have some brushstrokes and other uneven spots to remove to get a good flat surface. This should be done with the finest grade of abrasive which will do the job, ideally the micro grades if you have flatted back a couple of times already. Beware of cutting back right through the lacquer, which is easy to do on the corners. If you do, a matt area of slightly different colour this will reveal exposed timber.

Allow to dry thoroughly and recoat with several coats before leaving again to harden. Recoating can be done entirely without tidemarks with this type of lacquer.

When all surface features are removed, go down through grades of micromesh to 2400 at least and allow to dry before finally judging whether the surface is good enough to polish.

Polishing, or more properly burnishing, is done with a cream consistency buffing compound and a very great deal of 'elbow grease'. Soft cloth is needed; a couple of yellow dusters are ideal. Be aware that you can still go through the lacquer even at this stage. If you do, keep further buffing compound away from the area until it has been recoated.

The most unkind lighting conditions, and therefore the best for being critical about the finish you have achieved, is the other side of the room from a single window with no other lighting on.

BRIDGE FITTING

The position of the bridge will still be visible. Make sure that there is good finish right up to it. If you can obtain engraver's low or medium tack sheet, cover the entire bridge area and surround with it and press it down to exclude any air. You can proceed without it but it does make it easier not to mark the finish around the bridge.

Buffing lacquer is hard but rewarding.

Cover the bridge area with low-tack sheet …

… and scribe round the bridge with a scalpel.

Put the bridge in place, held firmly in accurate position and once again go round it with the point of a scalpel. Remember that you are trying to cut through all the finish but none of the wood. The scalpel line should be in exactly the same place as

129

Chisel the lacquer from the bridge area.

before. Then with a dogleg chisel cut away the finish on the bridge area. Check the bridge on its cleaned area.

With plane and/or abrasives, fit the bridge caul to the curved underside of the bridge. Place and hold it in position inside

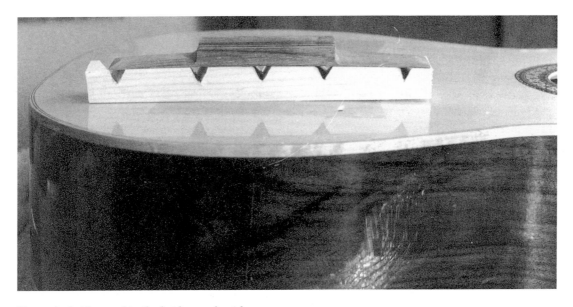

Shape the bridge caul to the bridge underside.

Screwing the bridge through into the caul.

the guitar with a couple of bits of double-sided tape.

Gluing bridges has always been a bit of a problem. They are very prone to slide on the glue layer with ordinary cramps. To overcome this, I recommend you to drill two holes in the tie block toward its front edge; ensure that these will not touch either the string holes or the fan strutting. With 25mm no. 6 screws with a ply washer under the head, screw them through into the caul underneath. Ensure that the bridge is still in place. This may sound a bit brutal but I have found no disadvantages and, clearly, from the marks on some famous old instruments it is not new.

This will hold the centre down and the bridge in place but will not press the wings into good contact, so bridge cramps are still needed. This is particularly so because you are putting water based glue on one side of a piece of timber 3–4mm thick. Inevitably it will bend by expansion of the wetted surface. You will need two upper cauls, therefore, to hold the wing edges down to the front. These can be fabricated from softwood with 4mm strips glued 20mm apart on a 30mm strip.

The cramps themselves rely on hardwood or thick ply strips and a couple of sections of the same square steel tube that you may use in the neck. Square tubing

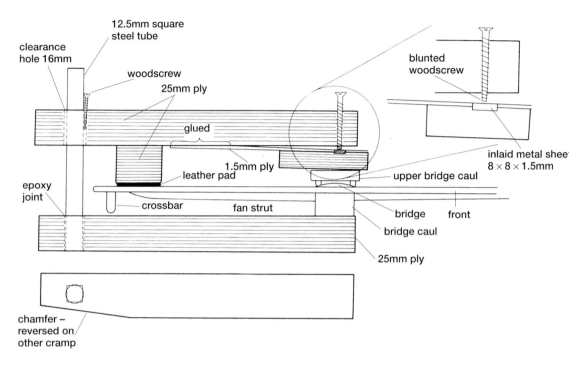

Fig 18 Bridge cramps.

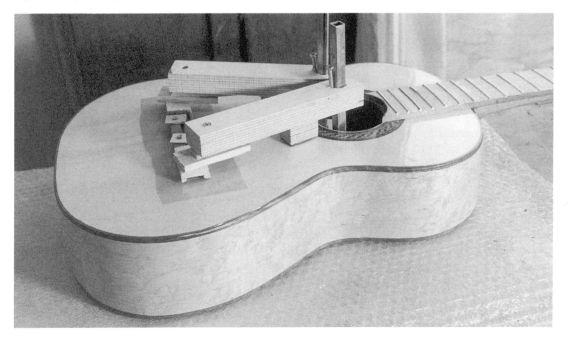

Bridge cramps in place.

Working on the tie block warrants another ply guard.

10mm wide is a press fit in a 12.5mm hole, and 12.5mm tubing fits a 16mm hole. The bottom joint may be epoxied but check that the assembly will go in through the sound-hole first. The upper member needs a clearance hole, best done by filing the corners of the hole a bit. Once assembled and pulled together, it is held in place with a screw between the steel tube and the side of the hole as shown.

All of this should be assembled dry to check the fit before it is all replaced with glue under the bridge. Use an even but very sparing layer of Titebond.

When all is dry and the cramps and screws are removed, the exuded droplets of glue are trimmed away with a dogleg chisel. This is where the layer of plastic sheet is so useful. You may choose to finish the bridge in the same material as the rest of the instrument but it can get marked during fitting, so you can leave it till now finally to smooth and finish its surface.

I usually finish to a very fine micro grit and wax, but lacquer is fine.

Styles of finishing the tie block are numerous and are designed to decorate and to protect from the constricting action of the strings, so hard materials are essential. You can lay on a thick veneer of a hardwood, e.g. Ebony, or of the nut and saddle material you are using. You can also buy a piece of Mother of Pearl for the purpose. You may prefer to rebate one of the above on to the front and back of the block and decorate the centre with spare pieces of the back and bits of rosette.

When you are satisfied that the bridge is finished you can remove the protective plastic sheet.

BRIDGE REMOVAL

In the unlikely event of a bridge moving during fitting or needing removal in a repair

Removing protective plastic sheet.

situation, ensure that there are no screws or bolts fitted. Protect the front with kitchen paper and pieces of drinks can. Place a line of craft-knife blades along the junction both sides, and with a pin hammer drive them between front and bridge to cut it off.

Bridge removal; usually a repair or major refurbishment procedure.

15 Stringing Up

In order to put strings on the guitar it is necessary to finalize the treatment of the frets, to make the nut and saddle and to fit the machine heads. This makes it sound simple but these include some highly skilled and subtle operations.

FRET DRESSING

Remove all masking tape and, using a craft-knife blade as a mini-scraper, remove any traces of lacquer from around the fret edges. There may be a hard and brittle edge to the lacquer at the sides of the neck. Take a fine abrasive emery-board and repeat the last fingerboard edge-filing operation (at 10 degrees) until the hard edge has gone. A little more edge burnishing will be necessary. To get the fret tops perfectly even, run a medium file blade across the top of the frets, keeping it parallel to the neck. With good overhead lighting, continue just until every fret has file marks across its top. This establishes an even height to the frets but a squared and marked top. Before proceeding further, protection for the fingerboard timber is necessary. Take two strips of drinks can metal with straight edges and tape them together with masking tape so that the space

Cleaning the edges with a mini-scraper.

Dressing fret tops.

Making a fret mask.

between is a fret width. Lay this over each fret before the following operations.

To start to round the fret top, run a file across the fingerboard both sides of each fret resting one edge on the fret and the other on the fingerboard guard. This takes the corner off the flat top. Take a piece of abrasive cloth and roll it into a tight cigar shape. Lay it alongside the fret and rub it back and forth, pressing it tightly against the fret. This rounds the filed flats on the fret. Proceed with grades of abrasive of around 120 to perhaps 400. Check the file marks on top of each fret against the light.

136

These must be removed but only by the penultimate grade of abrasive as they are your perfect height datum points. Work coarser abrasives according to the degree of remaining file marks. Each cigar of abrasive must be allowed to work round the end of the fret to take off the sharp filed square end. When this is completed to your satisfaction, put masking tape across the top of your fret guard and finish off with metal polish for an attractive finish. The masking tape prevents excess aluminium polishing swarf blackening everything.

Wash off the fingerboard with turpentine and rub it sparingly with petroleum jelly while still damp.

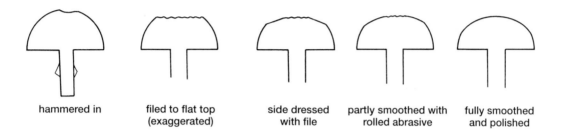

| hammered in | filed to flat top (exaggerated) | side dressed with file | partly smoothed with rolled abrasive | fully smoothed and polished |

Fig 19 Stages in fret dressing.

Taking the corners off the flat-filed tops.

At this stage, the machine heads can be fitted. The holes may need reaming out with the 10.5mm drill bit to remove any lacquer traces. If drilling for the screws beware of going into the string slots.

MAKING THE NUT AND SADDLE

The nut and saddle (and possibly decorative parts of the bridge) may be made of natural bone or Corian – a synthetic. Alternatively, junk shops may be scoured for old knives with ivory handles. You may find the materials respond better to a hacksaw or fine coping saw than one intended for wood.

The nut must be cut and filed to fit between the head veneer and the fingerboard and then shaped to the sides of the neck on each side. Neaten and square the head veneer with a chisel if necessary.

The nut must be slotted for the strings. File it until it stands about 3mm above fingerboard level and put a mark on its top 5mm from the edge of the treble side and 4–4.5 mm from the edge of the bass side. Divide the rest by five and mark the points.

(*Left*) Rounding with rolled abrasive fabric.

Cut and file the nut to drop between the fingerboard and the head veneer.

File into each of these marks with a fine triangular file to at least 1mm depth. Ensure that each slot tips back slightly towards the head. Leave this aside and move on to the saddle.

The saddle must be in firm flat contact with the bottom of its slot in the bridge, and a sliding fit. It will probably need to be higher on the bass side to give correct action both sides. For the moment, shape it so that about 5mm stands above the bridge right across.

THE STRINGS

Temporarily fit both E strings (*see* string fitting below) and tighten just until the string is taut. Measure the string height at fret twelve and compare this with what you planned in Chapter 10. For every 1mm you want to take off the height you must take 2mm off the saddle. Adjust it until it is still

1mm too high. As you get toward the end of this adjustment you need to put a smooth rounded shape on the saddle top. This can be done in such a way that the actual point of string contact can be controlled back and forth across the 3mm thickness. Mark each string position and shape with a file or a scraper. Treble E needs to make contact quite near the front edge of the saddle. G needs to be further back on the saddle with the saddle front cut away in rounding it, etc. (*see* the section on Compensation in Chapter 12). Leave this still a little too high and return to the nut.

The string must be in firm contact with the front edge of the nut. Any possibility of movement here wrecks tone. A triangular slot sloping back just enough provides good contact but not optimum tuning sensitivity. A round-bottomed slot improves string movement but any sloppiness at the front edge will cause 'fuzz' or 'buzz'. Probably the best string slot file is a wound

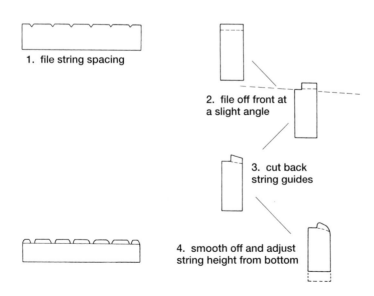

1. file string spacing

2. file off front at a slight angle

3. cut back string guides

4. smooth off and adjust string height from bottom

Fig 20 Stages in nut adjustment.

(*Above*) File away the front 2mm of the nut at a slight angle.

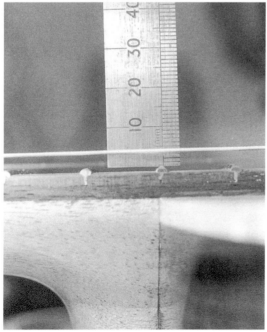

Adjust at both ends to correct fret twelve clearance. This is about 3.3mm – ideal student guitar setting.

string of correct diameter held taut but it is difficult to keep it from belling out both ends. My method is to file away the whole front 2mm or so of the nut once the string slots are initially cut. This is done at a slight angle. Then the string slots are cut to slope down from this level using needle files or wound string material. It is effectively turning the nut into a zero fret and string guide.

Final string height adjustment is done by judiciously filing from the bottom of the saddle and nut to obtain string heights of very slightly less than 1mm at the first fret and the values previously decided upon at fret twelve.

Having carefully set the compensation, its effectiveness will depend on string quality. Strings will only compensate correctly if they are of absolutely even diameter along

Fig 21 Attaching strings.

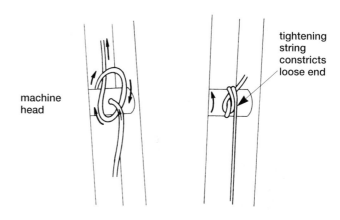

machine
head

tightening
string
constricts
loose end

insert strings from
saddle side – pull
through and form loop
around treble side.
Bass strings then loop
under, E once
      A+D twice.
Treble strings then
loop over, G once
      B+E twice

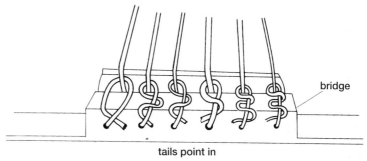

bridge

tails point in

their length. If in doubt about your choice of string, measure the treble monofilament strings with a micrometer at many places. This is worth doing to find a reliable make. Only then can you be sure that the octave at fret twelve is accurate. Note that the harmonic at fret twelve is bound to be accurate but will only sound clearly on accurate strings. Harmonic and note at fret twelve will be the same pitch only with suitable compensation and accurate strings.

It is important to install strings neatly and to trim ends as soon as up to tension to avoid spurious buzzes. Ensure that there is no excess string around the tuning capstan and that what is there is not about to bind against the woodwork. My suggestions about string windings are best given in diagram form. In the unlikely event of the first string slipping at the bridge and coming off, you may find that touching its end with the flat-iron is neater than tying a knot in it.

16 Further Challenges

Completing your first guitar will give you a sense of great satisfaction, inevitably qualified by those minor points where something did not go quite as hoped. I suspect that all woodworkers who make a guitar can be grouped into those who say 'never again' and those who are drawing up plans for the next almost before finishing the first. So, in a sense, you may already have an agenda for your second guitar based on your ideas of how well the first worked out. In this chapter I want to suggest ways in which subsequent instruments may advance beyond your first.

Do not imagine from this that the design I have suggested thus far is lacking sophistication. Contouring the front thickness; doming the front and its bridge fitting; linking bridge structure with fan strutting and many other details take you beyond the point where some of the literature on the subject has gone. However, there are still techniques which are aimed at teasing out an even better performance or adjustment of the instrument.

CONSTRUCTIONS OF SOME FAMOUS LUTHIERS

Studying the construction techniques of famous luthiers past and present soon reveals that they had many ideas about how to place and arrange the fan struts. Some of these are more complex than my basic five struts while some are completely different conceptually. Torres, of whom

you should read more elsewhere, consolidated this type of structure but made variations upon it.

The seven fan and two diagonal struts may be said to be his standard arrangement. The central five struts are exactly those I have suggested, surrounded by four others as shown in the diagram. Many have suggested at various times that the two diagonal bars are dispensable. I suggest that the outer fans are the least important but Torres included these nine and a large number of luthiers follow this.

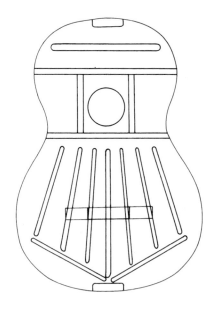

Fig 22 Torres' original seven-fan strutting. Still the commonest design.

Another Torres arrangement effectively vibrates a larger area of the perimeter of the lower bout by arching the cross strut to allow the fan struts to pass through it. Increasing the vibrating area enhances the volume but since it does not stiffen the central area, this can be at the expense of higher frequencies. This can lead to a mellowing of tone offsetting the carrying power of the greater volume. It depends on the tone you are aiming for.

Successful luthiers Kohno and Humphrey have opted to support the front with square crossed arrangements, but without

Fig 23 Another Torres design.

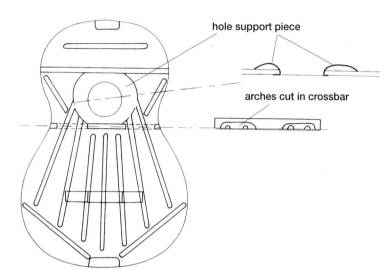

Fig 24 Kohno and Humphrey design (*below*).

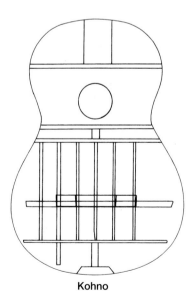

Kohno

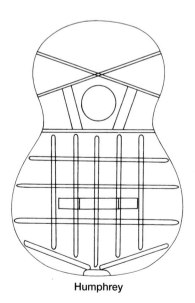

Humphrey

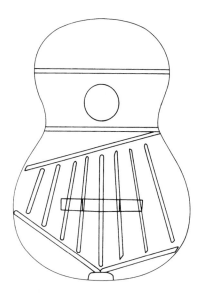

Fig 25 Generalized asymmetric design.

details of thicknesses and stiffnesses it is not easy to see the basis of their theories of spreading vibrations.

Asymmetric arrangements are many and try to satisfy the requirements of higher frequencies on the treble side of the front while bringing out lower frequencies on the other side of the bridge. Ramirez and Fleta are among the famous using asymmetric arrangements. I believe that vibrations spread in all directions from their point of origin but that higher frequencies die more quickly so need expressing nearer the bridge.

The cross-braced pattern given for steel-string guitars originated on gut-strung guitars. Carefully related to the wings of the bridge, it can still give a very nice sound to a classical instrument.

Studying these variations is limited by the lack of information which usually accompanies them with regard to front contouring, bridge thickness and the myriad other details with which an experienced luthier finely adjusts his instruments. Strutting arrangements alone are interesting but only a fraction of the picture.

THE BRIDGE

The weight and stiffness of the bridge make their contribution to the sound of the guitar. Since the bridge can be left unfinished until last it is quite possible (using two L-shaped guards in ply) to modify the thickness and taper of the wings and, moreover, to do this with the instrument strung up. The cabinet scraper will allow you to take material off the wings in a controlled fashion and to judge for yourself the effect of lighter, more flexible wings. Some idea of the effect of weight can be gained by adding Blue-Tack and small fishing leads. This can only increase your feel for getting the best sound out of bridge adjustment. It is really the only adjustment easily done after hearing the instrument.

THE FINGERBOARD

My suggested fingerboard surface is in a single plane. This is another standard design incorporated into many top-quality guitars. It is not the only approach, however.

The bass strings need a higher action because they vibrate further from the rest position than do lighter-weight strings. Vibrating against a fret causes metallic buzzing noises when trying to play passages with greater volume. It is possible to make the fingerboard thicker on the bass side of the nut but thinnest at the body end of the bass side. This allows higher action for the bass string without needing to build the bridge saddle higher on the bass side. This style of fingerboard front is effectively twisted along its length. Half a millimetre more thickness under bass E fret one and less under fret twelve is difficult to detect but makes a 0.75mm rise in action.

The bass strings that we are trying to keep from touching the frets vibrate not in straight lines but in a continuous curve. If we mount them high enough over the fingerboard so as not to touch fret twelve when vibrating, they are actually more likely to touch frets three, four or five if the fingerboard under them is flat. To make a concave curve in the fingerboard under the bass strings to match the curve of their vibration is called 'Bass relief'. It is relatively slight but is detectable by looking along the fingerboard down the bass side. It resembles warpage under string tension except that it doesn't occur on the treble side.

That classical fingerboards must be flat across their width is another convention increasingly challenged by some luthiers and by players who realize that barré work is facilitated by a crown on the fingerboard. This is more like the steel-strung guitar, although the doming is usually less with a radius of at least 50cm.

Thus we can build up a picture of a fingerboard with constant cross curvature, flat under the treble strings but concave under the mid/top of the bass side and with its thickest point at the bass side of the nut; thinnest at bass side fret twelve. This is a complex and subtle curve, not easy to execute to best effect and one which complicates fret dressing as this can no longer be done with a flat abrasive surface. If you wish to try this contouring, the scraper is your tool. Fret dress the bass side with a wooden emery-board of slight flexibility.

The fret dressing can also be modified slightly on the treble side by varying the angle at which the frets are filed back. Frets one to four can be filed back at 45 degrees, and this angle can then be increased to come vertical at fret twelve. This gives a smooth feel to the neck side where the fingers slide most often and decreases the chance of pulling a string over the side nearer the body where this is most likely to occur.

THE LOWER CROSSBAR

This can be fitted to the front when strutted and made straight. The front will then be stressed slightly when fitted to the straight front of the sides since the induced bow below the crossbar is pushed upward by the lower bout. Slightly better response is possible if the crossbar is not fitted until after the front – sides joint. After fixing front to sides, this crossbar will need a slight but accurate curve planed into it to drop on to neat contact with the front. This gives a smoother, longer dome to the front viewed from the side. Rib blocks are then essential.

SPLICING THE NECK

It is possible to create a centre splice in the neck, or the neck and head of a contrasting timber. This can be both decorative and strengthening. In splitting the neck down the centre, the opportunity can be taken to oppose the grain directions in the two halves and thus protect against warping.

Establishing a spliced joint the length of the head and neck takes a little longer and starts slightly differently. Before being separated, the neck and head (heel pieces removed) are cut along their length and one side is turned over or rotated to oppose the grain directions. This should result in any warpage effectively opposing itself.

Centre splicing the neck. Note the opposition of grain direction (Cedrela with Greenheart centre).

The two pieces are then tacked back together with glue without any attempt at a perfect joint. Then the head piece is separated off and scarfed back on as before. The splice is cut from some decorative and/or particularly rigid timber. Some have used Ebony; I have used flamed Maple or Greenheart with decorative black veneer sandwiching. The splice should be about 6–8mm wide and needs to be deeper than the neck piece. The centre piece is scarfed at the same angle as the head and neck but in the opposite plane. Veneer is most easily applied to it by covering the splice and the veneer with a film of Titebond and ironing it on with a hot flat-iron after the glue is dry.

The head – neck assembly is then sawn down its roughly glued centre line and trued up with a trying plane on its inner faces. The splice is assembled in the middle with all surfaces glued and is then held with the front and back faces of head and neck correctly aligned by the neck screw-cramps already mentioned. These have ply spacers on their faces to hold the neck timbers in alignment without interfering with the splice itself. Pressure has to be applied to the sides of the neck assembly with vice(s) and/or other cramps.

With great care, it is possible to veneer the head face first and have the centre splice coming like an inlay down the middle of the matching facing veneers. After planing off excess splice timber all round the procedure continues as before.

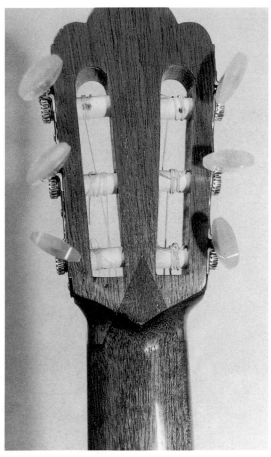

Another head joint. Traditional but not easy. No attempt is made to hide this join.

146

MAKING YOUR OWN ROSETTE

The complex and colourful parquetry rosettes available today are so cheap that it is not economical to try to make them as they contain thousands of pieces made from sizes of wooden strip that are not commercially available. Originally, rosettes were simply concentric arrangements of purfling and these are worth making for a slightly more 'period' look.

The arrangement of purflings is almost always symmetrical with one or three

(*Right*) 'Thousands of pieces ... of wooden strip that are not commercially available'.

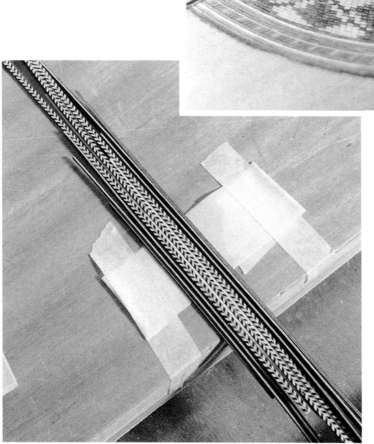

Plan purfling rosettes on upturned masking tape.

Work from the inside – it needs less pins.

(*Right*) Cut the last strip in by hand for the best fit.

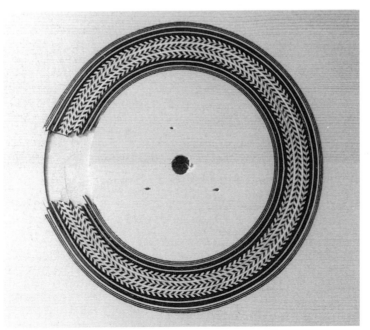

The final effect.

bolder patterns at the middle. Stick your strips to masking tape with sticky side up to plan the array. When these are assembled, measure the width; this would normally be between 16 and 24mm. Leave the channel just too narrow so that the last purfling on the outside needs cutting in by hand with a scalpel. Always work from the inside so the strips tend to pull in toward the glue. Dressmaking pins are used to hold the strips in while glue dries.

It is also worth trying bold geometric patterns as these can be built up in the same way as the commercially available rosettes and give an idea of what is involved. You need to build up the pattern in the centre area of the rosette as a long block probably about 10mm square and carrying your pattern like seaside rock. Once purfling layers are established on the inside of the channel, the block is sliced like salami about 1mm thick and slightly edge trimmed to fit evenly side by side. Finish off symmetrically with purfling. One example is illustrated. (A Japanese saw blade is very useful for this.)

A bold geometric look – and the 'salami' from which it was cut.

| To Make ... |

A TRAMMELLING ROUTER BASE

Channels for rosettes can be cut with the inlay cutter and chisel but for neatest results a trammelling router base is the answer. This is designed with one half that fits the router cutter opening and another that fixes to the guide bars by tightening up wood screws and carries the trammel pin as per the inlay cutter. These two balance the router level. Dimensions will need to be arranged to your own router.

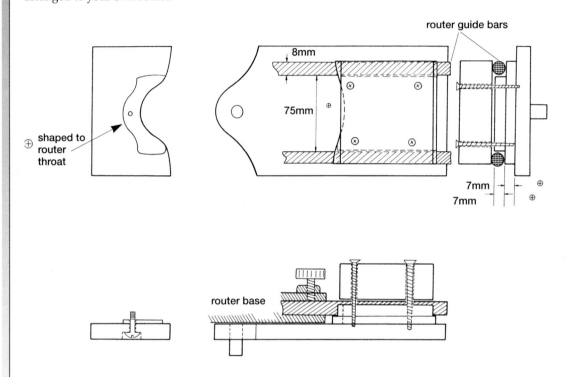

Fig 26 Wooden trammelling router base.

SHAPES

Varying the shape must be done with care and some sensitivity to the traditions and fashions which have grown up.

The standard shape I suggest is shown in Fig 27. For greater accuracy it can be given as a series of graph co-ordinates. A2 10mm graph paper will be needed.

0/0 0.1/3.0 0.4/5.0 1.0/7.0 1.9/9.0
3.0/10.4 5.0/12.1 7.0/13.0 8.0/13.3
10.0/13.4 13.0/13.0 15.0/12.4 16.0/12.0
18.0/11.5 19.0/11.3 20.0/11.4 21.0/12.7

The router trammel base – parts …

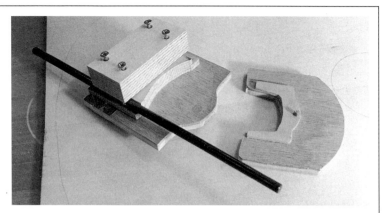

… and in operation.

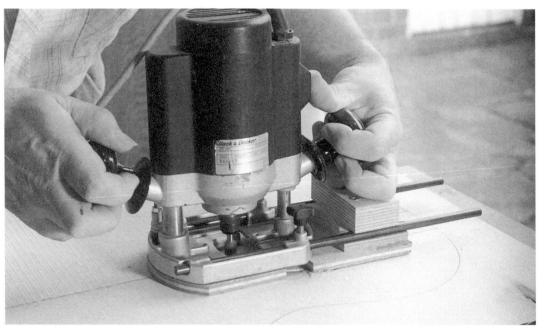

24.0/13.3 27.0/15.1 30.0/16.6 33.0/17.5
36.0/17.9 39.0/17.6 41.0/17.0 44.0/15.0
46.0/13.0 47.5/10.0 48.5/6.0 48.8/0

This is a slightly fuller and rounder shape, still in the tradition but a little more modern perhaps.

0/0 0.2/4.0 0.9/6.0 2.0/8.4 4.0/10.7
6.0/13.0 9.0/13.9 11.0/13.9 14.0/13.3
17.0/12.2 18.5/12.0 20.0/12.1 22.0/13.1
25.0/15.1 27.5/16.7 31.0/18.0 34.0/18.4
37.0/18.2 40.0/16.8 43.0/14.8 46.0/12.5
47.6/9.0 48.5/4.0 48.7/0

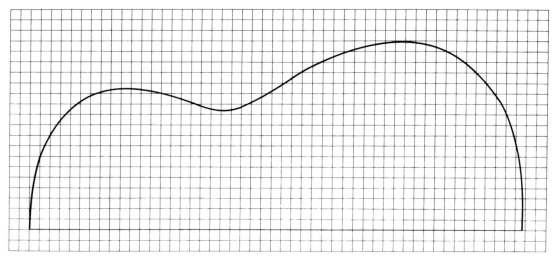

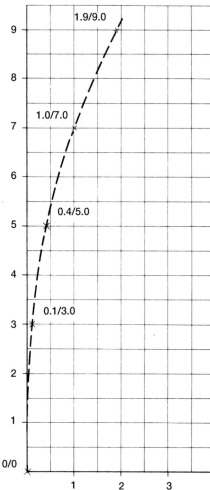

Fig 27 Shape on 1cm background (*above*).

Fig 28 Graphing shape figures 0/0 0.1/3.0 0.4/5.0
1.0/7.0 1.9/9.0 (1cm grid).

This is slightly square shouldered as a classical and rather larger but it is also acceptable as a steelstrung shape (*see* photo p.153).

0/0 0/3.0 0.3/7.0 1.0/9.0 2.0/10.8
4.0/12.5 7.0/14.0 9.0/14.2 11.5/14.0
15.0/13.1 17.0/12.5 19.0/12.2 21.0/12.8
26.0/15.4 31.0/18.0 35.0/19.0 37.0/19.1
40.0/18.6 43.0/17.3 46.0/14.8 47.4/13.0
48.5/10.4 49.0/8.5 49.5/0

For a smaller guitar, quite normal in Torres' day but rather a period novelty now. Best scale length probably 62–63cm (*see* photo p.149).

0/0 0.2/3.0 0.8/6.0 1.5/7.5 3.0/9.4
5.0/10.8 8.0/11.6 10.0/11.5 12.5/11.0
15.0/10.1 17.0/9.4 18.0/9.3 19.0/9.5
21.0/10.4 24.0/12.1 27.0/13.7 30.0/14.9
33.0/15.4 36.5/15.0 39.0/13.9 42.0/11.3
44.0/8.5 44.7/4.0 44.9/0.

17   The Steel-strung Guitar

All the same skills and basic methods described are needed in the making of a steel-strung guitar. The differences between the classical and steel-strung guitars exist for three reasons.

The string tension is much greater on a steel-strung guitar. The construction of the guitar is heavier and stronger for this reason.

The steel-strung guitar normally has its neck joining the body at fret fourteen. This

The differing geometries of classical and steel-strung guitars. Identical body shape (shape 3).

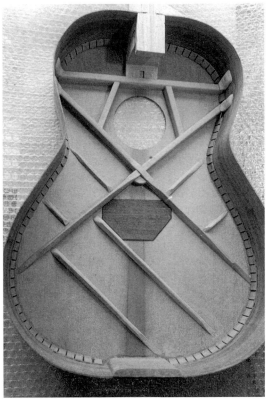

The steel-string bracing.

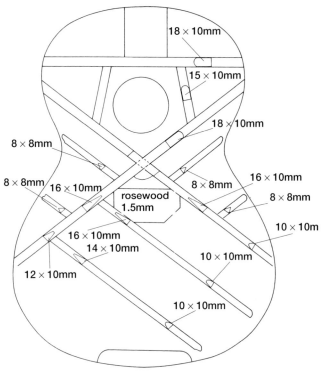

Fig 29 Suggested steel-strung strutting.
Timber – W. R. Cedar S. G. 0.34.

Details of the cross-halving
reinforcement.

154

means that the bridge is on a different part of the front, much nearer the hole, and this changes the whole geometry of the front construction.

The bridge is normally of the type where the strings pass down through the front and are held in place by bridge-pins. This precludes a 'fan strutting' type of body design as the holes would cut through the structural struts inside. Not all bridges are of this design and it is not uncommon to have a bridge which holds the string ball ends above the front. With this kind of bridge and a twelve-fret neck, classical-type fan strutting built more heavily produces a very fine sound.

CROSS BRACING

It is more normal to build the front to what is called 'cross bracing'. The main supports under the front are two similar struts from about the top of the hole level to the widest part of the lower bout, cross halved in the middle just below the hole and picking up the wings of the bridge as they diverge. Other strutting is added to provide further support and to spread vibrations. Patterns vary slightly but one such is illustrated and the strut thickness indicated. The cross halving joint can be strengthened with glue and fabric but I prefer to cut in a wooden strip to link across the opening of the halving joint and add an angled block of wood linking across the angle of the joint.

Under the bridge is a sheet of hardwood, in this case a piece of Indian Rosewood from a side, about 1.5mm thick, to resist the wear of the string ends.

The front is also thicker than a similar classical. The top bout and front of bridge area are about 3mm tapering off to 2.5mm around the lower bout edges. Backs are slightly thicker: 3–3.5mm according to density. The sides cannot really be made any more than 2mm without getting more difficult to bend.

The neck of a steel-strung guitar is narrower than a comparable classical but this is also more variable. Nut widths can be from 50mm down to 36mm. String spacing can be as narrow as 30mm at the nut but tend to be more standardized at the bridge where spacing is usually between 52–56mm.

The neck can be reinforced with square steel tube as I have recommended for the classical: 12.5mm material is probably best here. It is often the case that an adjustable truss rod is used in place of the simple reinforcement. The adjustable truss rod is put in very much as described for the non-adjustable. It has a nut at one end which can usually be put in the front of the head behind the nut and covered or inside the hole. When the nut is tightened the truss rod bends. It is set in so that it bends the neck

The adjustable truss rod from Luthier's Supplies. This is the underside when fitted.

backwards when tightened and this is done only if the constant tension of the strings has caused the neck to bend forward.

The fingerboard normally has a positive curvature but the amount of this is not standard. Care must be taken to achieve the same curvature all the way along or stings are very likely to buzz somewhere. A curvature template is useful: 35cm radius is a good starting point.

There are two kinds of machine heads. Those that fit slotted headstocks and look quite like the classical kind, but without the plastic 10mm sleeve around the capstan, are fitted as already described. Others fit from behind and protrude the end of their capstan through the front of the head. These may be three on one backplate or individual machines. Close attention must be paid to the thickness of the head to fit these correctly. They usually fit a thinner headstock, which can make hiding the scarf joint a slightly different operation.

The fitting of the neck – body joint in most steel-strung instruments is by a tapered dovetail joint into a wooden block in the top bout. This is a mass production technique, difficult by hand and with no advantages that I can see. I recommend the hand builder to proceed as per classical construction.

DECORATION

Bindings and purflings are mostly very similar to the classical guitar at the sides and back. Edge inlay is sometimes done in mollusc shell materials but this is extremely time consuming and I recommend more normal purfling. The rosette is dealt with differently. Simpler purfling rings are often incorporated around the hole; complex coloured rosettes are not. A compromise I can recommend as effective and

Head design. This tapered design keeps the strings nearer to a straight line at the nut.

easy is an annulus of bookmatched patterned veneer surrounded by purfling. This can be done in very much the same way as a rosette but bearing in mind how thin veneer is, more care must be taken in getting it flush with the finished surface.

Bridge (Makore), rosette (Lacewood) and pickguard (Burr Walnut) in a W.R. Cedar front.

The bridge design is less standardized and usually wider in the middle. If bridge pins are fitted, a tapered reamer is very useful. If a block is incorporated and drilled to hold ball ends above the front, it is tempting to drill and bolt down the bridge bottom edge and cover the holes with decorative dowels.

ACTION AND COMPENSATION SETTINGS

The 'action', i.e. string above fret height, is less for steel strings. Actions can be 2.5mm bass E/2mm Treble E or less. Players' preferences differ. In planning the action as in Chapter 10, you will probably find that with the thicker strutting, the doming of the front ends up slightly less with use of the same platen and that this tends to favour a lower action.

Compensation settings are also quite different with steel strings and, although the previous comments about approximation still apply, my suggestions are:

$$E = 4.5mm$$
$$B = 5.5mm$$
$$G = 5.0mm$$
$$D = 5.5mm$$
$$A = 6.5mm$$
$$E = 8.0mm$$

These can normally only be achieved by angling the whole saddle piece.

Suppliers

Luthier's Supplies
The Hall
Horebeech Lane
Horam
Heathfield
East Sussex TN21 0HR

One of very few suppliers of all instrument making necessities, not just wood.

North Heigham Sawmills
Paddock Street
(off Barker Street)
Norwich NR2 4TW

Suppliers of hardwoods and softwoods. Stocks of sawn guitar wood and finger-boards.

Timberline
Unit 7
58–66 Morley Road
Tonbridge
Kent TN9 1RP

Peter Lang and Bob Smith are both great enthusiasts and very knowledgeable.

Touchstone Tonewoods
44 Albert Road North
Reigate
Surrey RH2 9EZ

Suppliers of a wide range of instrument-making woods, accessories and tools.

Craft Supplies
Millers Dale
Nr Buxton
Derbyshire SK17 8SN

Increasingly stocking good instrument wood and many useful sizes and varieties of exotics. For instrument wood ask for Mark Hammock.

In America:

Stewart-Macdonalds Guitar Shop Supply
PO Box 1087
Bozeman
Montana 59715
USA.

Sell everything!

Index